KA-RUMBLE
RUMBLE
RUMBLE
RUMBLE

*Year 12 of the Taishō era.**

*The Taishō era spanned from 1912 to 1926.

The Great
Kanto
Earthquake

HH!
THUD
KA-
BAM
THUD
THUD
THUD
Sign: IMPERIAL THEATE

UGH.
WHAT A SHAME.

I QUITE LIKED THIS THEATER.

DE-FROTT!
AOI?
I KNEW I'D FIND YOU HERE!
GET OVER HERE!
IT'S DANGER-OUS--
AH!
CRAK
WHOOM

WHOOSH
WHY DID YOU COME?
WHY? TO SAVE YOU!
HA! A HUMAN, SAVE ME?
I'M A VAMPIRE, REMEMBER?

TRUST ME! I'LL GET YOU OUT OF HERE, EVEN IF IT'S THE LAST THING I DO!
......
JUST GIVE UP ON ME.

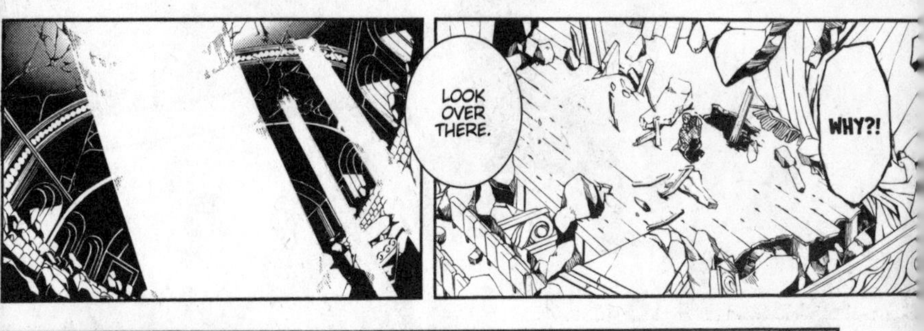
WHY?!
LOOK OVER THERE.

IF IT WAS DARK OUT, THIS MEASLY EARTHQUAKE WOULD POSE NO PROBLEM, BUT IT JUST *HAD* TO HAPPEN DURING THE DAY.
AT THIS POINT, EVERY VAMPIRE IN THE IMPERIAL CAPITAL WILL BE WIPED OUT.

AND HONESTLY, I'M TIRED OF LIVING LIKE THIS. I'VE LONG HAD MY FILL.
SHAKE
HAH!
HAH!
SHAKE
HOW STUPID!
YOU CAME EVEN THOUGH YOU'RE TERRIFIED!

AND NOW YOU HAVE NOWHERE LEFT TO RUN.

WHEN I REMEMBERED THERE WAS A CHILD ALL ALONE IN THIS DARK THEATER...
I HAD TO COME.

I'M NO CHILD!
THAT'S WHAT ALL KIDS SAY.

I'LL HAVE YOU KNOW THAT I'M THE **OLDEST** VAMPIRE!
ONLY STUPID LITTLE BRATS SAY THEY'RE TIRED OF LIVING.
WHOOSH
AOI!

DAMN.
TODAY'S REALLY NOT MY DAY.
GRAB
!
SHUTARO...

BWOOSH!

KEPT YOU WAITING, HUH?

Several years earlier.
During the early 20th century, when Western powers competed for dominance...
the era of Taishō romanticism bloomed across Japan.
竹本福龍
Banners: Takemoto

Imperial Capital
Ladies and gentlemen enjoyed elegant evenings.
The masses spent their time in cafés, chatting about the latest European trends.
And intellectuals became the stars of this new culture.
Tokyo

A NEW PLAY IS OPENING IN ASA-KUSA!
A FOREIGN BOY'S IN IT, RIGHT
SQUEAL
SQUEAL
However, even in this bright new world, there are shadows.
Evil forces that no one has noticed yet.

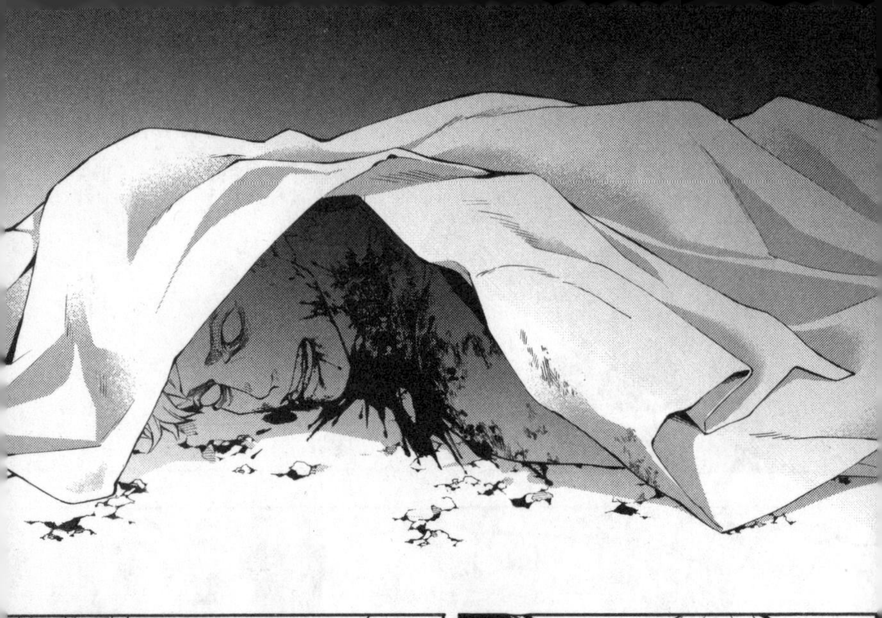

STAY BACK FROM THE CRIME SCENE, MISS!
URK!

IT'S THE SAME AS LAST TIME!
HIS THROAT WAS RIPPED OUT, TOO!
CHATTER
CHATTER
YOU HAVEN'T CAUGHT THE KILLER YET?!
GOOD GRIEF!
CALM DOWN! A RABID DOG DID THIS!!

GOD, I HATE RUBBER-NECKERS!
SO, WHAT'S THE STORY?
SAME AS USUAL.

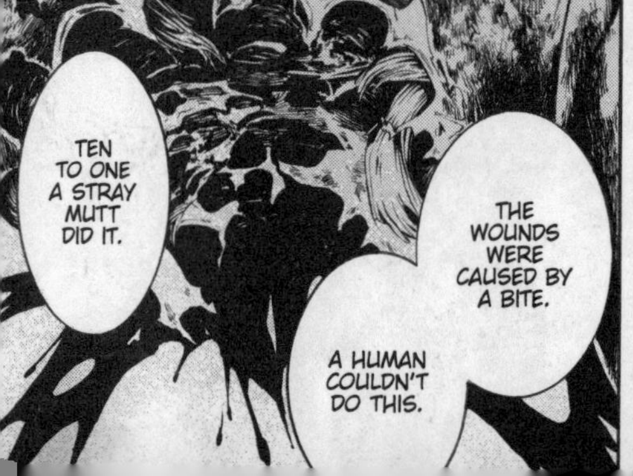
THE WOUNDS WERE CAUSED BY A BITE.
A HUMAN COULDN'T DO THIS.
TEN TO ONE A STRAY MUTT DID IT.

IS THAT *REALLY* THE CASE?
!

HEY, MISS!
GET BACK!
I'VE MAPPED OUT THE OTHER ATTACKS. THIS IS THE SECOND INCIDENT TODAY.
AND EVERY SINGLE BODY WAS DISCOVERED IN THE CITY CENTER.
THERE WASN'T A **SINGLE COMPLAINT** ABOUT WILD DOGS BEFORE THESE INCIDENTS BEGAN.

WHAT IF THESE ATTACKS ARE **MURDERS** AFTER ALL?
WHA?!
Hey!
DON'T LISTEN TO SOME AMATEUR!
WHO SAID I WAS AN AMATEUR?
BEAM
OH! ARE YOU A DETECTIVE?!

I'M SHIRASE AOI!
A REPORTER FROM THE NITTO NEWS! IT'S A PLEASURE TO MEET YOU.
Nitto News

Hmm!
GREAT. THEY WON'T LET ME INSPECT THE CRIME SCENE.
OH, AOI-CHAN!
PLAYING REPORTER AGAIN?
YOU'RE THE LADY FROM THE PHOTO STUDIO!
I'M NOT "PLAYING"! I MAY BE A NOVICE, BUT I'M STILL A PROFESSIONAL!
DON'T POKE YOUR NOSE TOO DEEP INTO DANGEROUS AFFAIRS, YOU HEAR?
Ha ha

HAS SHUTARO-KUN WRITTEN YOU YET?
I SEE. I HOPE YOU GET WORD FROM HIM SOON.
SO DO I.

SHUTARO...

YOU'RE MOVING DANGEROUS GOODS?!
Don't worry. It's a simple transport job. Should be pretty boring, honestly.
I still don't like it.
Trust me.
I promise I'll come back alive.
......
More importantly, what's this about you working at the news-paper?
You always said you wanted to uncover hidden truths.
I'm sure you'll do a great job!

Notice of Death
Army: Private First-Class
Kurusu Shutaro
Time Minutes
30 Day hour (AM) (PM)
illed in action (during battle) May 30th
A...
death notice?
日本駐屯地
Is Kurusu Shutaro really dead?!
It can't be!
If you've received a death notice, then it's true.
But it doesn't even list his place of death or his unit!
You expect me to *accept* this?!
Sign: Japanese Garrison
Go home.
Aoi-chan.
I under-stand how you feel, but there's nothing you can do.
CLENCH

They never sent us his body!
Why is everyone so quick to believe some worthless scrap of paper?!

BACK WHEN MY BROTHER'S DEATH NOTICE ARRIVED...

SHUTARO HELD ME AS I SUNK INTO GRIEF.

I'VE ALREADY LOST TOO MANY PEOPLE.

COME BACK HOME, SHUTARO.
YOU PROMISED, REMEMBER?

DON'T LEAVE ME ALL ALONE.
STRETCH
UGH!
I CAN'T BREAK DOWN LIKE THIS!
A GOOD REPORTER NEEDS AN IRON WILL! C'MON, AOI!
SHLIP
BLOOD ?!
GASP!

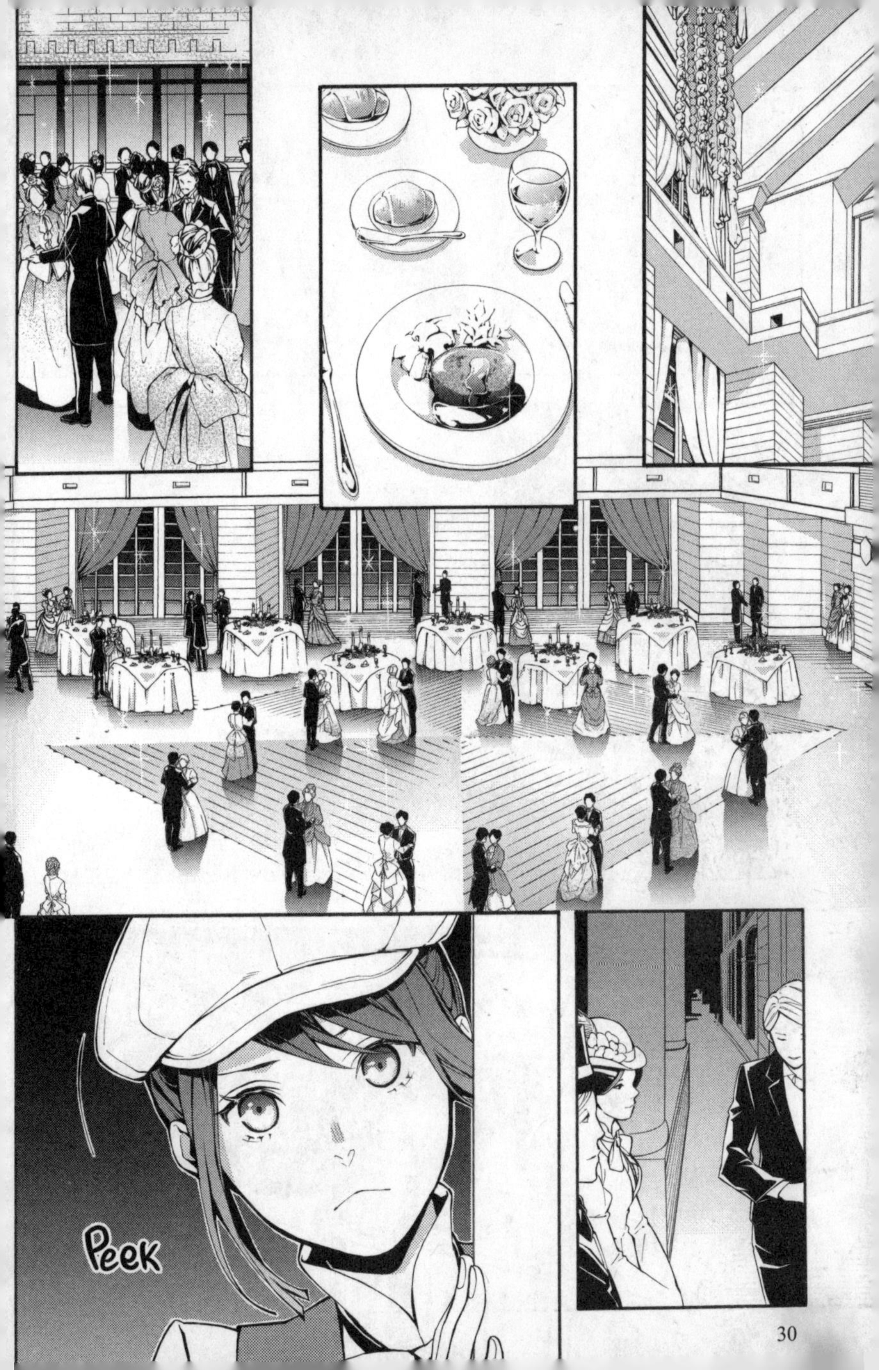
Peek

I FOLLOWED THE TRAIL OF BLOOD...AND IT LED ME TO A FANCY HOTEL!
I stick out like a sore thumb.

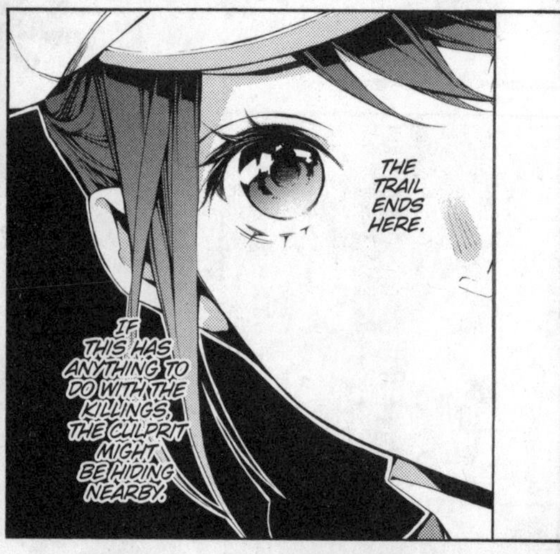
THE TRAIL ENDS HERE.
IF THIS HAS ANYTHING TO DO WITH THE KILLINGS, THE CULPRIT MIGHT BE HIDING NEARBY.

THE POLICE...
A dog did it.
Go home.
......

I'LL HEAD TO THE SECURITY ROOM, THEN--
Tap

THUNK
AH!
SORRY!

WHAT'S THIS?
STAAAARE
UMM...? EXCUSE ME.
STARE
STARE
STARE
STARE
HUH? WHAT IN THE WORLD?!

AM I IN DANGER?!
STAA
GRIN
GUESS NOT.
Phew!
YOUR SKIN IS EVER SO PALE AND LOVELY!
CRIMSON BLOOD WOULD STAND OUT QUITE NICELY ON YOU.
OKAY, I **AM** IN DANGER!

CALM DOWN, AOI! AS A JOURNALIST, I CAN'T MAKE FALSE ASSUMPTIONS.
MAYBE HE'S JUST BAD AT TALKING TO PEOPLE?
WH-WHAT DO YOU MEAN?
THAT I'D LOVE TO USE YOU AS A TEST SUBJECT, OF COURSE!
NOPE, HE'S CRAZY!!!!
TA--
KE--
U--
CHI--
THWAM
AH.

GRAH!
THE HELL ARE YOU DOIN'?!
DIDN'T I TELL YA TO STICK BY ME?!
I'M *NOT* AFRAID!!
DON'T BE AFRAID. I'D NEVER LEAVE YOU, YAMAGAMI-SAN.
WHAT NOW?

SADLY, I MUST GO.
BUT LET'S MEET AGAIN SOON...
MY LITTLE GUINEA PIG! ♪
HIS WHAT?
PLEASE KEEP IT TOGETHER. WE'RE ALL COUNTING ON YOU.
NGH.
DON'T TELL MAEDA.
WHAT WAS THAT...?
!
FWSH

DASH
COULD THOSE TWO BE--?!
HUH?

THWAM
AH...!

EEK!
DEAD BODIES ?!
BA-THUMP

ZWIP
BAM

RED EYES?!
......!
GRK
GRK
GRK
WHAM

IT'S NOT HUMAN!
HAH!
HAH!
HAH!
YOU'RE THE KILLER, AREN'T YOU?

I'LL GET THE POLICE!
DASH

!

N-NO!
GR
AH!

WHAM
GAAH!
SKRSSSH
Y-YOU!
THE MAN FROM EARLIER--

GET THE HELL OUTTA HERE, YA IDIOT!!!
GR
O-OKAY!
GRAB
GAH!

RIP
RIP
GAAH!
RIP
DAMMIT!
LET GO!
SQUEEEZE
WHAM
LET GO OF HIM!!
RIGHT NOW!
YA IDIOT!

WHACK
GAAAH!
RIP
RIP
RIP
RIP

AH!
AHH!
AH!

GAH!
SOMEONE...
SOME-ONE HELP HIM!!

BWOOSH

SORRY I'M LATE.

SLUMP...

FWISH

YOUR LEGS GAVE OUT ON YOU, HUH?

IF YOU'RE GOING TO WATCH THIS PLAY, HERE'S A FRONT ROW SEAT.
A STAGE FIGHT IS ABOUT TO BEGIN.
THREE OF THEM?
BUSY NIGHT.
GRRRA!

SHK

THAT ONE'S YOURS.
SWIPE
THWAM
GRIP
!
SHLP
SHLP
SHLP

YANK
HEH!

WHAM

TWITCH
TWITCH

AGGH!
!
ZWSH
QUIT FOOLING AROUND.

AT LEAST *TRY* TO BE GENTLE, TAKEUCHI!!

CUT THE DRAMATICS.
WE HARDLY FEEL PAIN, REMEMBER?

AFTER ALL, WE'RE THE SAME BREED OF MONSTERS AS OUR ENEMIES.

I ALMOST FORGOT! DON'T KILL THEM!
I NEED THEM FOR MY EXPERIMENTS!

HUH?
NO...

MY PRECIOUS SPECIMENS!
NOOOOOO!
THEY AREN'T WORTH CRYING OVER.

STILL!
STAND BACK.
WHAT'S THE PLAN, TAKEUCHI? WE'RE OUT OF TIME.
WISH

TOSS
THIS IS OUR ONLY OPTION, THEN.
CLICK
!
KA-WHOOOOSH
CONSIDER YOURSELVES LUCKY.

I SHALL GRANT YOU A VISION OF DAWN IN YOUR FINAL MOMENTS!
SOMETHING WE CAN NEVER ENJOY, NO MATTER HOW MUCH WE DESIRE IT.

WHOOSH

!
!
ARE YOU ALL RIGHT?!
FLINCH
HUH?
WH-WHAT?!
YOU'RE HURT!
CAN YOU STAND?!

WHERE DID THE MASKED GUYS GO?

WAS IT A DREAM?
NO, THAT'S IMPOSSIBLE!

ARE THEY...?
YES. THEY'RE FROM THE ARMY.

IT SEEMS THEY SHOT A MOVIE HERE LAST NIGHT.
APPARENTLY, SOME EQUIPMENT MALFUNCTIONED AND DAMAGED THE BUILDING, SO THEY'RE HERE TO DO REPAIRS.

A MOVIE?
THAT'S RIGHT! WAIT, WERE YOU AT THE SITE OF THE ACCIDENT?
I HEARD THE FIGHT SCENE WAS AMAZING.
Too bad I missed it...
WHAT DOES ALL THIS MEAN?

I'LL BE ON MY WAY, THEN.
WAIT, PLEASE!! WE WERE NEVER INFORMED OF ANY MOVIE SHOOT!

ALL YOU NEED TO KNOW...
IS THAT THIS MATTER IS NOW AN OFFICIAL INQUIRY BY CODE ZERO, THE 16TH GARRISON OF THE JAPANESE IMPERIAL ARMY'S MILITARY POLICE.

SHUT UP.
BE A GOOD BOY AND ACCEPT IT.
Mutter
HUH?!
WHAT DID YOU SAY?!

CODE ZERO?!
EH?! MISS!
FWUMP
THERE WAS NO MOVIE SHOOT!
IT WAS ALL REAL!
CODE
THE RED-EYED MON-STERS.
THOSE MASKED MEN.

AND...
Sorry I'm late.
THAT VOICE...

IT WAS SHUTARO'S!
Whew!
THAT WAS...
THE NIGHT I FIRST LEARNED ABOUT CODE ZERO.

OH MY!
SO THERE'S A GROUP LIKE THAT IN TOKYO?

First Night
Too Deep Into the Night

CLANK

CLANK

CLANK

CLANK

This is a tale of vampires and humans.

MARS RED

MARS RED

Siberia.
BWAM

Where are they?!
Keep your head down!
ZWISH
Huff!
Huff!
Huff!

Huff!
Huff!

Over there!
Shoot!
Kill him!
BA-BAM

Hah!
Hah!
BA-
BA-
BANG
Hah!
Hah!
Hah!

ZWO
OSH
AAAAAAH!
DRIP
CRUNCH

CRUNCH
CRUNCH

Ngh.

GRAB

SHWOO

?

They're gone?

Second Night
Code Zero

I'D PREFER TO DIE, IF THAT'S OKAY.
NOT AN OPTION. DRINK UP!

BUT IT'S BLOOD!!
GOT THAT RIGHT! IT'S THE ONLY DAMN THING WE CAN STOMACH!
GULP
?!
YA WON'T DIE IF YA DON'T DRINK IT, BUT YA'LL SHRIVEL UP LIKE A DRIED FISH!
I HATE DRIED FISH.
LOOK, JUST IMAGINE IT'S SOFT-SHELLED TURTLE BLOOD.
BUT I HATE SOFT-SHELLED TURTLES, TOO.
YOU PUNK...
US VAMPIRES ARE THE COUNTRY'S SUPER SOLDIERS.
Sigh!
GIMME A BREAK ALREADY.
JUST ACCEPT THAT WE'RE NOT HUMAN.

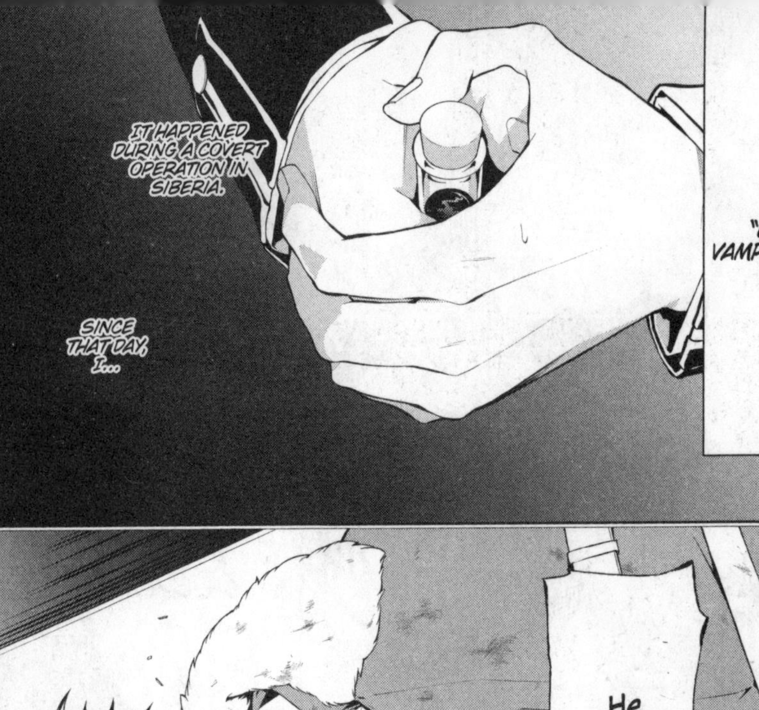
"US VAMPIRES."
IT HAPPENED DURING A COVERT OPERATION IN SIBERIA.
SINCE THAT DAY, I...

He got bit?!

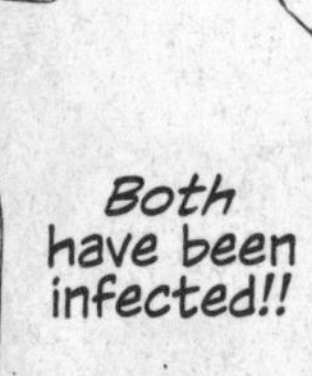
Yes!
The vampires we were transporting got free and nearly annihilated the entire unit!
Only two people survived!
RATTLE
RATTLE
Major Yamagami from the military police and Private First-Class Kurusu!
RATTLE
Both have been infected!!

What's the rank of their sire?
An unranked and an S-class, respectively!

GLOOM...
An S-class?!
Which one?!
Which one did the S-class bite?!

Private Kurusu Shutaro.

Move them to the basement.
That unit can manage them.

The 16th Garrison of the Japanese military police

A K A

Code Zero

"YOU'RE A VAMPIRE NOW" DOESN'T CUT IT. I NEED ANSWERS!
THE MINUTE WE WOKE UP, THEY TOLD US TO JUST DO AS WE'RE TOLD AND HUNT DOWN MONSTERS EVERY NIGHT!
WHAT THE HELL IS THIS?!
HOW ARE YOU OKAY WITH EVERYTHING, YAMAGAMI-SAN?!

SOLDIERS MUST OBEY ORDERS.
BUT...
WHAT, YOU GONNA TURN TRAITOR?

WHAT ABOUT YOUR WIFE?
ARE YOU REALLY ALL RIGHT LEAVING HER?
THEY TOLD EVERYONE WE DIED.

I BET SHE'S BAWLING HER EYES OUT RIGHT NOW.
HMPH.
SHE'S A SOLDIER'S WIFE. SHE KNEW WHAT SHE WAS IN FOR.
LOOK ON THE BRIGHT SIDE.
IT'S KIND OF COOL BEING A VAMPIRE, ISN'T IT?
HOW?! WE'RE NOT MUCH DIFFERENT FROM HUMANS. WE'LL STILL DIE IF WE GET SHOT.
Glare
OH? DO YOU WISH TO TEST THAT THEORY?

BLAM
NO!
FWUMP

OW!
WHO THE HELL JUST SHOT ME?!
YOU'RE ALIVE!

Hee hee hee...
SEE? HE'S NOT DEAD.
VAMPIRES ARE AMAZING, AREN'T THEY?
TAKEUCHI!

BLAM
BLAM
OW!
GAH!
STOP!
THAT HURTS!

CUT THAT CRAP OUT!
IT MIGHT NOT KILL ME, BUT IT STILL HURTS!!
UH, GOOD MORNING.
OH, YES. GOOD MORNING.
SL IDE
WHOA!

THIS IS LANCE CORPORAL TAKEUCHI OF THE MILITARY POLICE. HE'S THE HEAD OF THE SCIENCE AND TECHNOLOGY DEPARTMENT.
WHAT'S THAT?
MY LATEST INVENTION. IT'S STILL TOO STRONG.
I WANT TO LEARN MORE ABOUT HUMAN MUSCLES. MAYBE I CAN SLICE YOU OPEN LATER?
NO WAY.
WHEN HE WAS INTRODUCED TO US AS A MEMBER OF CODE ZERO, I FIGURED HE WAS JUST AN AWKWARD GUY, BUT...

TURNS OUT, HE'S A TOTAL WEIRD-O.
HUH? YOU HAVEN'T HAD BREAKFAST?

I STILL CAN'T BRING MYSELF TO DRINK THIS.

PERHAPS TASTE AND SMELL ARE MORE SENSITIVE IN YOU RARE ADVANCED-CLASS VAMPIRES.

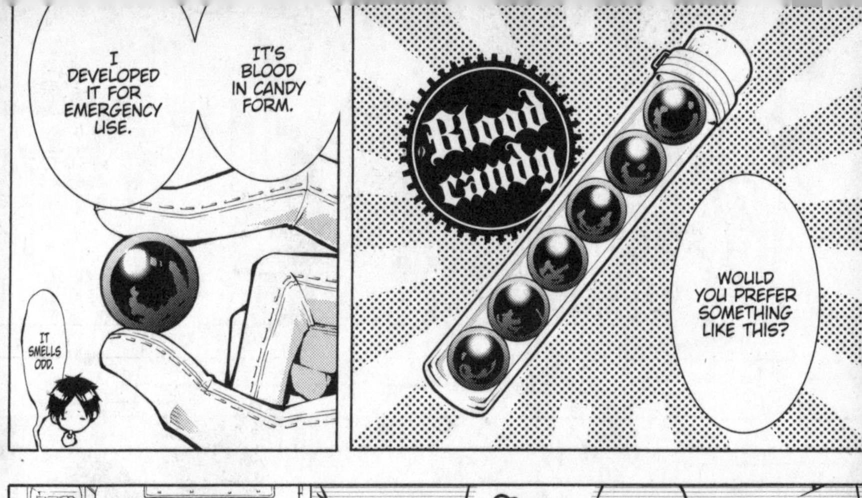
WOULD YOU PREFER SOMETHING LIKE THIS?
Blood candy
IT'S BLOOD IN CANDY FORM.
I DEVELOPED IT FOR EMERGENCY USE.
IT SMELLS ODD.

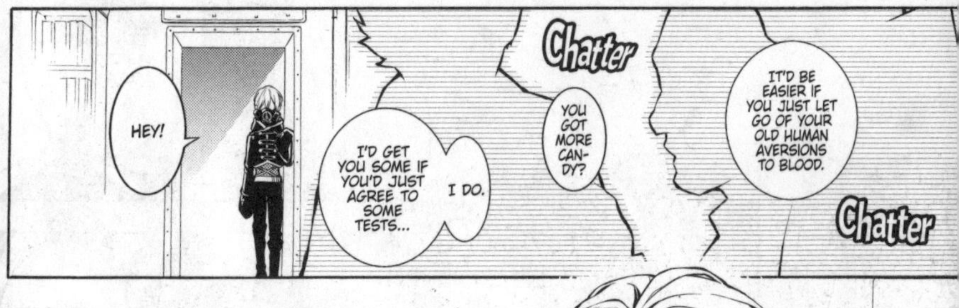
Chatter
IT'D BE EASIER IF YOU JUST LET GO OF YOUR OLD HUMAN AVERSIONS TO BLOOD.
YOU GOT MORE CAN-DY?
Chatter
I DO.
I'D GET YOU SOME IF YOU'D JUST AGREE TO SOME TESTS...
HEY!

THE CAPTAIN'S CALLING US.

CORPORAL SUWA!
GOOD DAY TO YOU.
WHAT ARE YOU GUYS DOING?

THAT MEANS ALL HIS INJURIES HAVE HEALED, I ASSUME?
SEEMS SO.

RIGHT! WE HAVEN'T MET THE CAPTAIN YET!

HE'S PROBABLY SOME DAMN UPSTART FROM ICHIGAYA.*
Hmph!
I'LL WHIP HIM INTO SHAPE!

THE CAPTAIN OF CODE ZERO...
I WONDER WHAT HE'S LIKE.

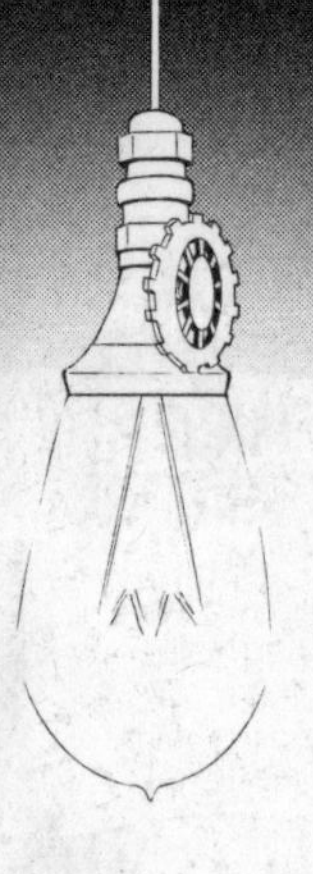

WHAT WILL HE ASK OF US?

*The Japanese Imperial Army's general headquarters was located in Ichigaya during the Taishō era.

BAM
I'M COLONEL MAEDA YOSHINOBU!
HENCEFORTH, YOU LOT IN CODE ZERO ARE UNDER MY COMMAND! WE WILL USE YOUR VAMPIRIC ABILITIES TO CARRY OUT SPECIAL OPERATIONS!
OUR MAIN DIRECTIVE IS TO SEARCH FOR ANY VAMPIRES HIDING IN TOKYO THAT MAY ATTACK HUMANS...
AND EITHER RESTRAIN OR DISPOSE OF THEM!
SO THIS IS COLONEL MAEDA.

Glare
WHAT'S WRONG, YAMAGAMI?
IS THERE SOMETHING ON MY FACE?

WHY DOES IT GOTTA BE *YOU*, OF ALL PEOPLE, MAEDA?!!
UGH!
COLONEL MAEDA TO YOU.

DO YOU KNOW EACH OTHER?

WE WERE IN SCHOOL TOGETHER.
I SURPASSED YOU IN RANK, WHILE PRIVATE KURUSU OVER THERE SURPASSED YOU IN VAMPIRE CLASS!
HOW IRONIC.

MAEDA
!!!
MAEDA?

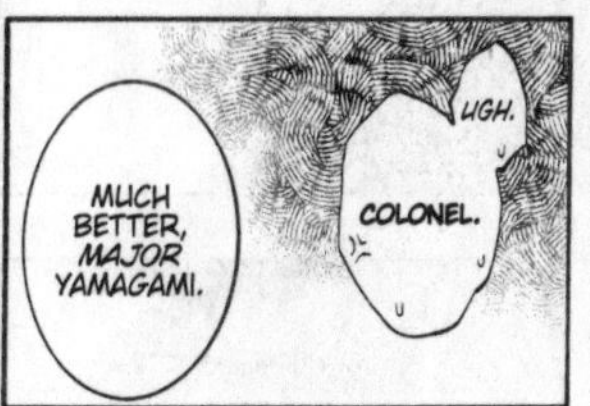
UGH.
COLONEL.
MUCH BETTER, MAJOR YAMAGAMI.

That damn hick!
MUTTER
KURUSU SHUTARO.
THE ONLY A-CLASS VAMPIRE IN JAPAN, THE SIRE OF AN S-CLASS.
YOU SURE DON'T LOOK LIKE MUCH.

I'M *NOT* MUCH.
BUT AMONG US, YOU'RE THE LEAST HUMAN, CORRECT?

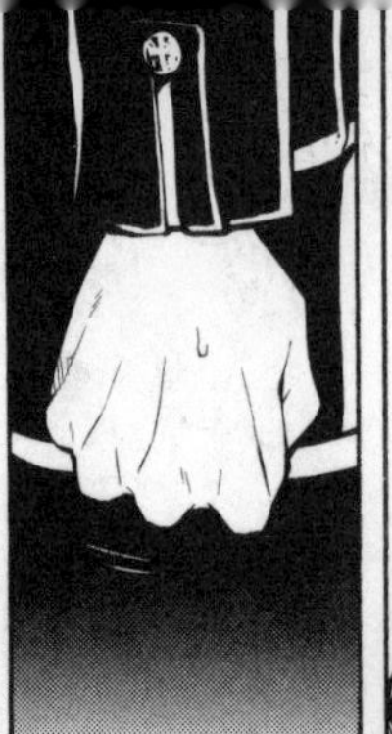

WE'LL HAVE YOU MAKE FULL USE OF THOSE ABILITIES IN THE FIELD.
SO, WHO IS OUR NEXT TARGET?

UM!
CAN'T WE HANDLE THINGS PEACE-FULLY?

WHAT?
I MEAN, IF THEY'RE ANYTHING LIKE US, CAN'T WE JUST TALK TO THEM?
THAT WAY, THEY WON'T ATTACK US LIKE LAST TIME.

TAKEUCHI.
Fwp
Sigh...
LISTEN, ALL VAMPIRES ARE MAJOR THREATS TO HUMANS.
THEIR BODILY FLUIDS ARE POISONOUS. APPROXIMATELY NINETY-NINE PERCENT OF HUMANS DIE WHEN EXPOSED TO THEM.
SHUDDER
POISON-OUS?
SO WE GOT LUCKY?

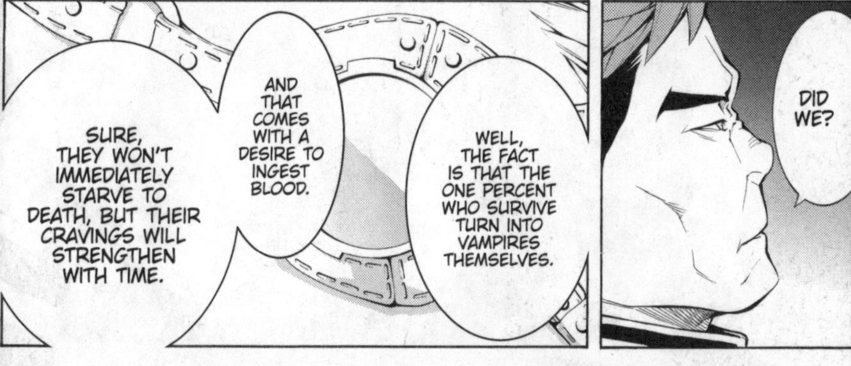
DID WE?
WELL, THE FACT IS THAT THE ONE PERCENT WHO SURVIVE TURN INTO VAMPIRES THEMSELVES.
AND THAT COMES WITH A DESIRE TO INGEST BLOOD.
SURE, THEY WON'T IMMEDIATELY STARVE TO DEATH, BUT THEIR CRAVINGS WILL STRENGTHEN WITH TIME.

......
IF THEY INGEST BLOOD THAT'S BEEN SPECIALLY PREPARED, THERE ISN'T ANY PROBLEM.
HOWEVER, ONCE THEY HAVE A TASTE OF FRESH HUMAN BLOOD, THE CRAVINGS TAKE OVER.
THAT'S WHY WE CAN NEVER TRULY REASON WITH THEM.

OUR ONLY OPTION IS TO KILL THEM.
YOU DON'T HAVE TO SOUND SO EAGER ABOUT IT!
IF POSSIBLE, BRING THEM IN ALIVE! I NEED MORE TEST SUBJECTS!
I'm begging you!
IF THEY CAN COMMUNICATE, WE'LL CAPTURE THEM.
THOSE ONES CAN JOIN THE ARMY.
AND IF THEY CAN'T?

KILL THEM.

NOW, ON TO THE MAIN TOPIC.
OUR NEXT MISSION...

VAMPIRES USUALLY BLEND IN WITH THE CROWD AND DON'T REVEAL THEMSELVES. OUR LAST MISSION WAS A RARE CASE.
SO HOW DO WE SPOT THEM?

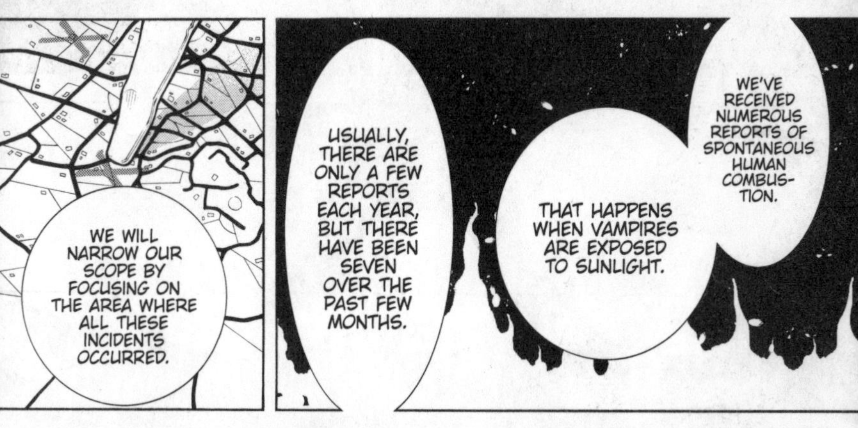
WE'VE RECEIVED NUMEROUS REPORTS OF SPONTANEOUS HUMAN COMBUS-TION.
THAT HAPPENS WHEN VAMPIRES ARE EXPOSED TO SUNLIGHT.
USUALLY, THERE ARE ONLY A FEW REPORTS EACH YEAR, BUT THERE HAVE BEEN SEVEN OVER THE PAST FEW MONTHS.
WE WILL NARROW OUR SCOPE BY FOCUSING ON THE AREA WHERE ALL THESE INCIDENTS OCCURRED.

WHAT A WASTE! VALUABLE TEST SUBJECTS LITERALLY GOING UP IN SMOKE!
CAN I ASK SOME-THING?
BACK OFF!
AGAIN?!
NO, YOU BACK OFF, UNRANKED.
WHAT IS IT, KURUSU?

IF THIS IS SUCH A WIDESPREAD ISSUE, SHOULDN'T THERE BE A TON OF PEOPLE DYING OF POISON?
WHY CAN'T WE LOCATE THOSE BODIES?
TRUE.
IT'S POSSIBLE THAT SOMEONE IS PREPARING THE BLOOD OR CONCEALING THE CORPSES.
A PLACE THAT HANDLES BLOOD?
LIKE A BUTCHER SHOP OR HOSPITAL?
OH! OR MAYBE THAT PLACE!

WHAT PLACE?

天満屋
Sign: TENMANYA

Asakusa.
NEVER THOUGHT I'D FIND A KEIAN IN THIS NECK OF THE WOODS.
A KEIAN IS A TYPE OF EMPLOYMENT AGENCY, RIGHT?
RIGHT. WE SURE THEY'LL EVEN BE OPEN THIS LATE?
ACCORD-ING TO TAKEUCHI, THEY ARE.
PARDON US.

WHOA!

INCREDIBLE!
IT'S FULL OF IMPORTED GOODS.

A CEMBALO, HUH? HAVEN'T PLAYED ONE IN AGES.

WAIT, *YOU* CAN PLAY IT?
Y'KNOW, YOU'RE PRETTY DAMN RUDE.

PLEASE DON'T TOUCH.
IT'S FRAGILE DUE TO ITS AGE.
A CHILD?
YOU'RE TAKEUCHI-SAN'S COMRADES, YES?
WE ARE.
I HEAR THIS PLACE DEALS IN INFORMATION.
CORRECT.
TAP
FROM DAYTIME CUSTOMERS TO NIGHT-TIME CUSTOM-ERS...
ALL THE INFORMATION VAMPIRES DESIRE IS HELD WITHIN TENMANYA.

I'M TENMANYA SHINNOSUKE.
I AM THE OWNER OF THIS SHOP.
Mumble
THANK YOU FOR STOPPING BY.
Mumble
YOU'RE THE OWNER?
YA SURE WE'RE AT THE RIGHT PLACE?
IF YOU DON'T BELIEVE ME, YOU MAY LEAVE.
BY SOME TWIST OF FATE, MY FAMILY HAS BEEN ON GOOD TERMS WITH THIS COUNTRY'S VAMPIRES FOR GENERATIONS.
Mumble Mumble
OUR JOB IS TO HELP THEM LIVE PROPER LIVES.
Mumble Mumble

DOES THAT MEAN YOU KNOW HOW VAMPIRES GET THEIR HANDS ON SPECIALLY TREATED BLOOD?

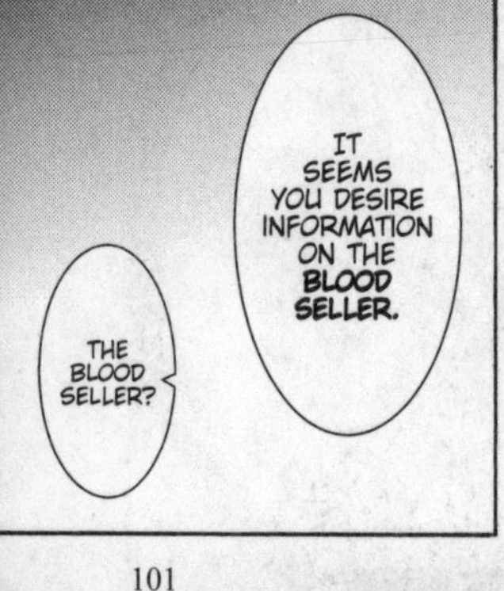
IT SEEMS YOU DESIRE INFORMATION ON THE **BLOOD SELLER.**
THE BLOOD SELLER?

AS IMPLIED, IT'S SOMEONE WHO SELLS BLOOD.
Mumble mumble
OR MORE SPECIFICALLY, BLOOD THAT CONTAINS SODIUM CITRATE FOR BLOOD TRANSFUSIONS, WHICH KEEPS IT FROM CLOTTING.
Mumble mumble
BEFORE THEY APPEARED, MY FAMILY HAD A MONOPOLY ON THE MARKET.
HOLD UP! SO YA KNOW WHERE THEIR HIDEOUT IS?!
NO.
AND EVEN IF I DID, I WOULD NOT TELL YOU.
THE HELL?!
YAMAGAMI-SAN, YOU'RE YELLING AT A CHILD.
IF A MERCHANT EVER SELLS OUT A CUSTOMER, THEY WON'T BE IN BUSINESS LONG.
THAT IS THE ONE LINE HERE AT TENMANYA WE WILL *NEVER* CROSS.
HOW-EVER...
Mumble
TAP...
IT IS FINE TO SELL OUT A **BUSINESS RIVAL.**

RECENTLY, SOMEONE NEW HAS COME ONTO THE SCENE.
I'M NOT CERTAIN WHO THEY ARE, BUT...

WHAT?

THIS IS A BUSINESS TRANSACTION, YES?
FOR SALE

YAMAGAMI, GIVE ME EVERYTHING YOU HAVE.
ME?!
YOU DIDN'T BRING *ANY-THING?!*
KURUSU!
WHY ME?!

THAT WAS A JOKE.
CRUSH-ING MY BUSINESS RIVAL WILL DO AS PAYMENT.

......
DING-DING
ISHIKAWA.
BRING *THAT* HERE.

ARE YOU ALSO A VAMPIRE?
NO.
BUT THEN... WHY HELP VAMPIRES?
YOU THINK IT'S STRANGE THAT I ALLY WITH MONSTERS?
NO...
IN MANY WAYS, HUMANS ARE FAR WORSE, DON'T YOU AGREE?
!...
ARE YOU FRESH BLOOD?
YOU STILL HAVE THE EYES OF A HUMAN.

SUPERHUMAN STRENGTH, ENDURANCE, AND RESILIENCE.
VISION THAT ALLOWS YOU TO SEE FAR INTO THE DISTANCE, EVEN AT NIGHT.
AN ABNORMALLY KEEN SENSE OF SMELL AND HEARING.
MUMBLE MUMBLE
AT A GLANCE, VAMPIRES SIMPLY SEEM LIKE SUPERIOR BEINGS...
BUT THEY HAVE *FAR* TOO MANY WEAK-NESSES.

YOU CANNOT SURVIVE ON YOUR OWN.

IT'S BEST TO REMEMBER YOU NEED PEOPLE LIKE ME TO LIVE IN THIS WORLD.

......

MASTER.
THANK YOU, ISHIKAWA.

LET'S CIRCLE BACK TO THE PREVIOUS TOPIC.
TAP
YOU'RE LOOKING FOR THE BLOOD SELLER, CORRECT?
WHAT'S THIS?
MY BUSINESS RIVAL'S TOOL.
Mumble...

MARS RED

MARS RED

Third Night
The Ryōunkaku

The Ryōunkaku
of Asakusa.
凌雲閣
Sign: Ryōunkaku

MY, OH MY, WHAT A MARVELOUS VIEW!

THEY SAY A SPRING VIEW IS WORTH A THOUSAND PIECES OF GOLD, BUT I THINK THAT'S UNDER-SELLING IT.

IS THAT FROM A PLAY?
OR ARE YOU A POET, SUWA-SAN?

Tch!
SO, WHAT NOW?

THERE'S BEEN NEWS OF A VAMPIRE SIGHTING.
RIGHT NOW, TAKEUCHI-SAN AND YAMAGAMI-SAN ARE SEARCHING BELOW.
DID YOU MISS THE PART WHERE THEY TOLD US TO PROVIDE BACKUP ONCE THEY FIND THEM?

UGH!
CAN'T WE JUST RUSH IN AND STRIKE FIRST?

WE CAN'T RISK CAUSING A SCENE WITH SO MANY PEOPLE AROUND.

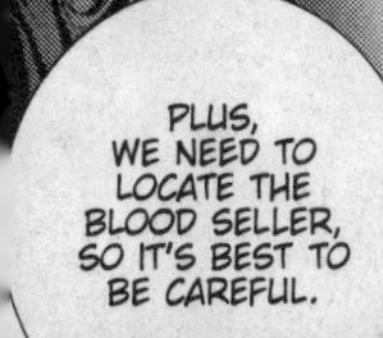
PLUS, WE NEED TO LOCATE THE BLOOD SELLER, SO IT'S BEST TO BE CAREFUL.

OH YEAH?
BESIDES, WE CAN'T BE SURE THEY'RE OUR ENEMY YET!
WE WON'T EVEN NEED TO FIGHT IF WE CAN TALK IT OUT.
THEY'LL NEVER SIDE WITH US.
THEY'RE LIKE ME. AND WE DON'T LIKE BEING KEPT ON A LEASH.
THEN WHY ARE YOU WORKING WITH US, SUWA-SAN?

BECAUSE I LOVE IT.
HUNTING *THEM*, I MEAN.

Buddhist Scriptures
Bookstore
Kawabata Ko
Mori Ougai
......

TAKEUCHI, DON'T LEAVE MY SIDE!
I'M SICK OF YOU ALWAYS DITCHIN' ME!
DON'T WORRY, I WON'T.
UGH! WHY AM I ALWAYS IN FRONT LIKE SOME KINDA DECOY?!

WE HAVE NO CHOICE.
I MEAN, YOU'RE THE ULTIMATE VAMPIRE TRACKER!
Vampire Class
Unranked
D
C
B
A
Scary!
AS A SURVIVAL MECHANISM, VAMPIRES CAN INSTINCTUALLY SENSE THOSE OF A HIGHER RANK THAN THEM!!
I DON'T GET WHY.
YOU CAN DETECT ME, BUT I CAN'T DETECT YOU!
IN OTHER WORDS, YOU CAN DETECT ANY VAMPIRE BECAUSE YOU'RE THE *WEAKEST!!*
← Unranked
D-rank→

BEEP
YOU'RE THE SUPREME VAMPIRE DETECTION DEVICE, THE YAMAGAMI RADAR!
DON'T CALL ME THAT!
BOY, WE'RE SO LUCKY THAT YOU BELONG TO THE LOWEST RANK!!
TCH! THIS IS A HELLUVA LOT SCARIER THAN I EXPECTED...
SHUDDER
THEY'RE HERE!

CHECK YOUR TEN.
HE'S WEARIN' BLACK AND HAS A HAT ON. THE GUY WITH GLASSES.
CHASE HIM TO POINT B!
TMP
AH!
THEY'RE ON THE MOVE. LET'S GO!
WHAT'S THE PLAN AGAIN?
ACT LIKE HUMANS...
AND FIGHT LIKE THEM, TOO.

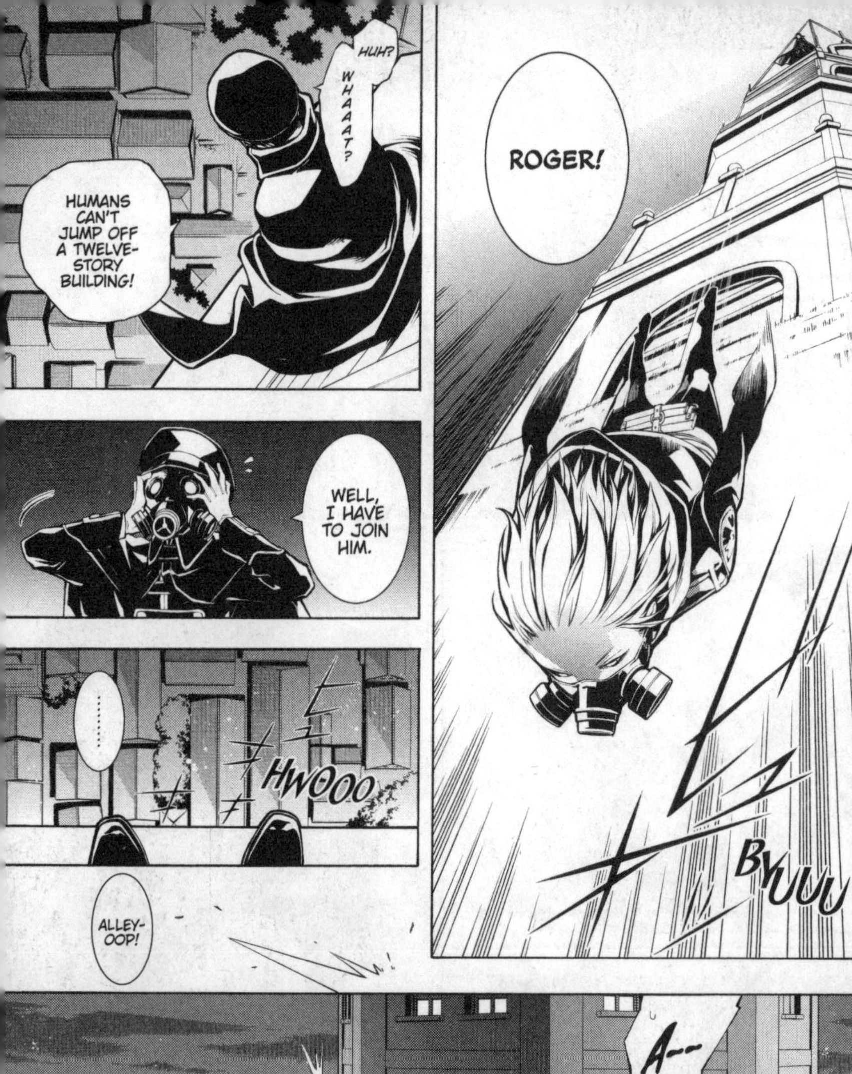

ROGER!
BYUUU
HUH?
WHAAAT?
HUMANS CAN'T JUMP OFF A TWELVE-STORY BUILDING!
WELL, I HAVE TO JOIN HIM.
......
HWOOO
ALLEY-OOP!

A--
H--
H--
H--
HHH!

HAH!
HAH!
HAH!

DEFINITELY A VAMPIRE.
I'M YAMAGAMI TOKUICHI OF SPECIAL UNIT 16!
YOU GOT TWO OPTIONS!

ONE! COMPLY WITH US. IN EXCHANGE, WE'LL PROVIDE YOU A SUPPLY OF BLOOD AND A FAMILY REGISTER.
TWO! REFUSE AND D--

BWOOSH
WHOA!

I'M NOT DONE WITH MY SPIEL!!
RIP
RIP
RIP
SEEMS NEGOTI-ATIONS HAVE FAILED.
TAKEUCHI! AIN'T YOU GONNA HELP?!
HOLD ON JUUUST A MINUTE. MY NEWEST CREATION IS...
Huh? Where did it go?
THWSH
GRRR!
YAMAGAMI-SAN! HOLD OUT FOR A BIT LONGER!
YOU NUTS?! I'M A GODDAMN UNRANKED VAMPIRE!
I'M SCREW-ED!
GRAH!
AHH! AHHH!

ZWSH
ARE YOU OKAY, YAMAGAMI-SAN?!
KURUSU! WHY ARE YA ALWAYS SO DAMN SLOW?!
SORRY! IT TOOK SOME TIME TO DROP OFF A TWELVE-STORY BUILDING.
TMP
YOU BEAT ME HERE!
......
SCUFF
OH? HE'S PARALYZED.

MISTER A-CLASS IS SOMETHING ELSE, ISN'T HE?
HE'S JAPAN'S FINEST FOR A REASON~!
Amazing!
YEAH.
BUT...
!
ANOTHER VAMP!
DASH
WAIT, HE'S--!
GET HIM!

WHAM
FWUMP
QUIT PLAYING AROUND.
C-COLONEL MAEDA?
CAPTURE THEM BEFORE THEY CAUSE A SCENE.

HMM?
ROLL...
THIS MAN ISN'T A VAMPIRE.

I SEE. SO, YOU'RE SAYING THE SECOND PERSON WAS A BLOOD SERUM MULE?
Lieutenant General Nakajima Sonosuke.

YES, SIR.
WE JUST SO HAPPENED TO INTERRUPT HIS TRANSACTION WITH A VAMPIRE.
TALK ABOUT GOOD TIMING.

IT SEEMS HE NEVER KNEW MUCH ABOUT THE SERUM OR THE CLIENT.
UNFORTUNATELY, THE MAN'S A SIMPLE SMUGGLER. HE ONLY EVER KNEW ABOUT THE DESIGNATED DROP-OFF LOCATION.

I'LL PERSONALLY INTERROGATE THE VAMPIRE. HOPEFULLY, I CAN EXTRACT SOME INFORMATION QUICKLY.

NO, TAKE CARE OF THAT LATER.
THERE ARE MORE PRESSING MATTERS.
SIR?

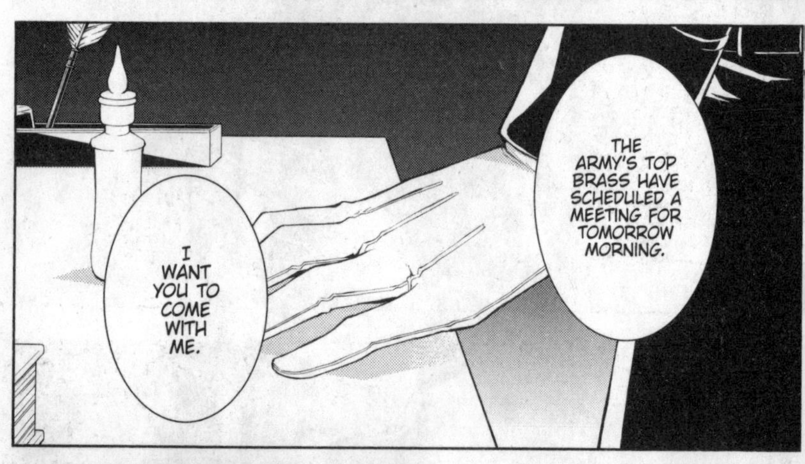
THE ARMY'S TOP BRASS HAVE SCHEDULED A MEETING FOR TOMORROW MORNING.
I WANT YOU TO COME WITH ME.

ME, SIR? BUT WHY?

IS THAT BACK TALK?
NO, SIR!
I'VE ONLY COME THIS FAR THANKS TO YOU...
LIEUTENANT GENERAL NAKAJIMA.
PLEASE USE ME, CODE ZERO, AND EVERYTHING ELSE YOU'VE CREATED AS YOU SEE FIT.

SHEESH!
NO NEED TO BE SO FORMAL!

GOOD WORK TODAY.
日都新聞社
Sign: Nitto News
WOW, IT'S SO LATE!
THERE'S AN EDITORIAL MEETING TOMORROW AND...
IMPERIAL THEATER
Romeo and Juliet
By William Shakespeare
Juliet
Romeo
Price for Two Seats
OH!
A POSTER FOR THE IMPERIAL THEATER'S NEW SHOW?
THEY'VE GOT SOMETHING NEW, HUH?
and Juliet
By William Shakespeare
They kept rerunning Salome until now.

DID YOU ENJOY *SALOME* THAT MUCH, MISS?
HUH?
YOU LOOKED DISAPPOINTED WHEN YOU SAW THE POSTER FOR *ROMEO AND JULIET*.
AH!
YOU!
et
Romeo
Defrott
YOU'RE *ROMEO* ?!
......
I'M SORRY! IT'S JUST... YOU LOOK LIKE THE PERFECT ROMEO!
"WHAT'S IN A NAME? THAT WHICH WE CALL A ROSE BY ANY OTHER NAME WOULD SMELL AS SWEET."
Romeo and Juliet By William Shakespeare
WOW!
IS THAT LINE FROM THE PLAY?!
INDEED! YOU MAY CALL ME ROMEO OR ANYTHING ELSE, DEAR JULIET.
AMAZING!
I'M A HUGE FAN ALREADY!

GLAD TO HEAR IT.
THAT OUTFIT... ARE YOU A DETECTIVE OF SOME KIND?
A REPORTER, ACTUALLY. I'M SHIRASE AOI FROM THE NITTO NEWS.
NITTO NEWS REPORTER
SHIRASE AOI
Tokyo
Nitto News
An Actress's Affair
Her Secret Lover
Nessie in Tokyo Bay?!
AH, YES. THAT NEWSPAPER RUNS RATHER *INTERESTING* ARTICLES...AND OUTLANDISH RUMORS.
WE *ARE* A TABLOID, AND WE *DO* PUT SOME EYE-CATCHING HEADLINES ON THE FRONT PAGE...
BUT I'M ONLY AFTER THE TRUTH!
HMM. YOU'RE QUITE HONEST.
WHY WORK AT THE NITTO NEWS, THEN?
THAT TABLOID IS A TERRIBLE PLACE FOR AN EARNEST GIRL LIKE YOU.
I'M LOOKING FOR SOMEONE... MY CHILDHOOD FRIEND WHO NEVER RETURNED FROM SIBERIA.
IF I KEEP CHASING AFTER THE TRUTH, I'LL FIND HIM EVENTUALLY.
AT LEAST, THAT'S WHAT I BELIEVE.
WHAT'S HIS NAME?

KURUSU.
SHUTARO--
HUH?!
WHAT'S WRONG?
I...

SHUTARO!!!
DASH
SORRY!
EXCUSE ME!
SHUTARO ?!
BA-THUMP
SHUTARO!
BWSH
HUH?

EH?
YOU...?

TH-THERE WAS ANOTHER PERSON WITH YOU JUST NOW, WASN'T THERE?!
A TALL, PALE GUY IN THE SAME UNIFORM AS YOU!

UH?
NOPE. THIS IS OUR ENTIRE GROUP.

ARE YOU LOOKING FOR SOMEONE?
Y- YES.

DO YOU KNOW SOMEONE NAMED KURUSU SHUTARO? HE'S IN THE ARMY, TOO!

SORRY, BUT ONLY THE THREE OF US ARE ON DUTY.

MUST HAVE BEEN A TRICK OF THE LIGHT OR SOMETHING.

I IMAGINED IT?
BOTH TIMES...?
I...
I SUPPOSE SO.
YOU LOOK PALE. GO HOME AND REST.
OR, COME BE MY GUINEA--
GAH!
YANK
WE'RE BUSY, SO PLEASE EXCUSE US.
NO CLUE WHO YOU'RE LOOKING FOR, BUT HE ISN'T HERE. JUST FACE THE FACTS.

HEY!
SOUNDS LIKE YOU'RE LOOKIN' FOR SOMEONE WHO AIN'T COMING BACK.

HE...
MAY BE GONE.

BUT ALL I WANTED WAS TO SPEND MORE TIME WITH HIM!

I MIGHT BE STICKIN' MY NOSE WHERE IT DON'T BELONG...
YOU DEFINITELY ARE.
I'M A SOLDIER, TOO.
I'VE WATCHED AS MY MEN DIED. I DON'T KNOW WHEN I'LL GO, EITHER.

BUT EVERYONE THINKS OF THEIR LOVED ONES AT THE END.
AND WE ALL WISH FOR THEM TO GO ON AND LEAD LONG, HAPPY LIVES.

SO, DO THAT.
THAT'S THE ONLY WAY HE'LL EVER REST IN PEACE.
SO YOU'RE SAYING...
JUST ACCEPT THAT HE'S DEAD?

I'M SAYIN' YA GOT A BRIGHT FUTURE, BUT ONLY IF YA MOVE ON.
NO POINT LYIN' TO YA NOW. IT'D JUST MAKE THE HURT WORSE LATER.
THANK YOU.
SORRY FOR BOTHERING YOU.
UM!
PLEASE DON'T DIE!
LIVE A LONG, HAPPY LIFE SO YOU CAN RETURN TO YOUR LOVED ONES, ALL RIGHT?!

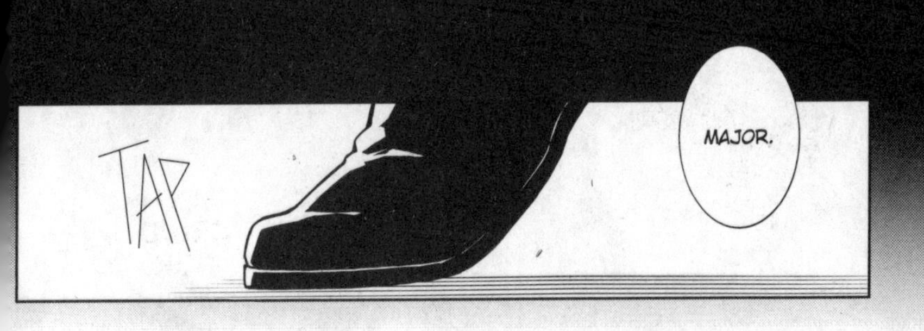
MAJOR.
TAP

THANK YOU FOR DOING THAT.

HMPH. I DIDN'T DO NOTHIN'!

NO.

YOU CRIED FOR ME.

ARE YOU ALL RIGHT?

DEFROTT?
SORRY I RUSHED OFF LIKE THAT.
DO YOU KNOW THOSE MEN?

NO! IT WAS A MISUNDER-STANDING.
ANYWAY, IT'S LATE. I'LL WALK YOU HOME.

HEY.
DO YOU KNOW THEM?
PLEASE. TELL ME MORE.
DROOP
SURE...

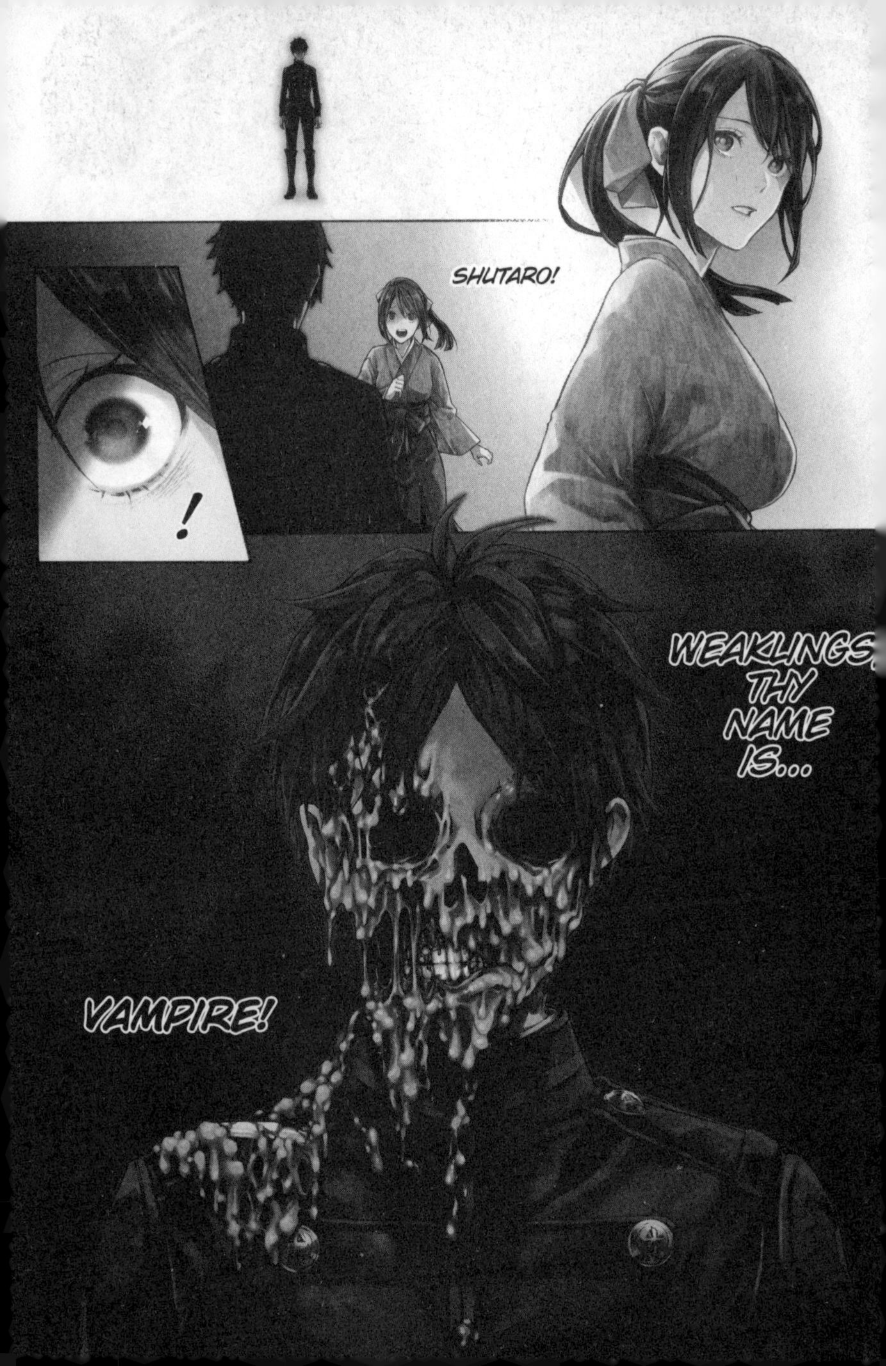

SHUTARO!

!

WEAKLINGS, THY NAME IS...

VAMPIRE!

Fourth Night
Operation: See You in Your Dreams

MARS RED

SHUTARO!!!
Hah
Hah
Hah
A DREAM?
WHEN...
CHIRP CHIRP CHIRP
DID I GET HOME?

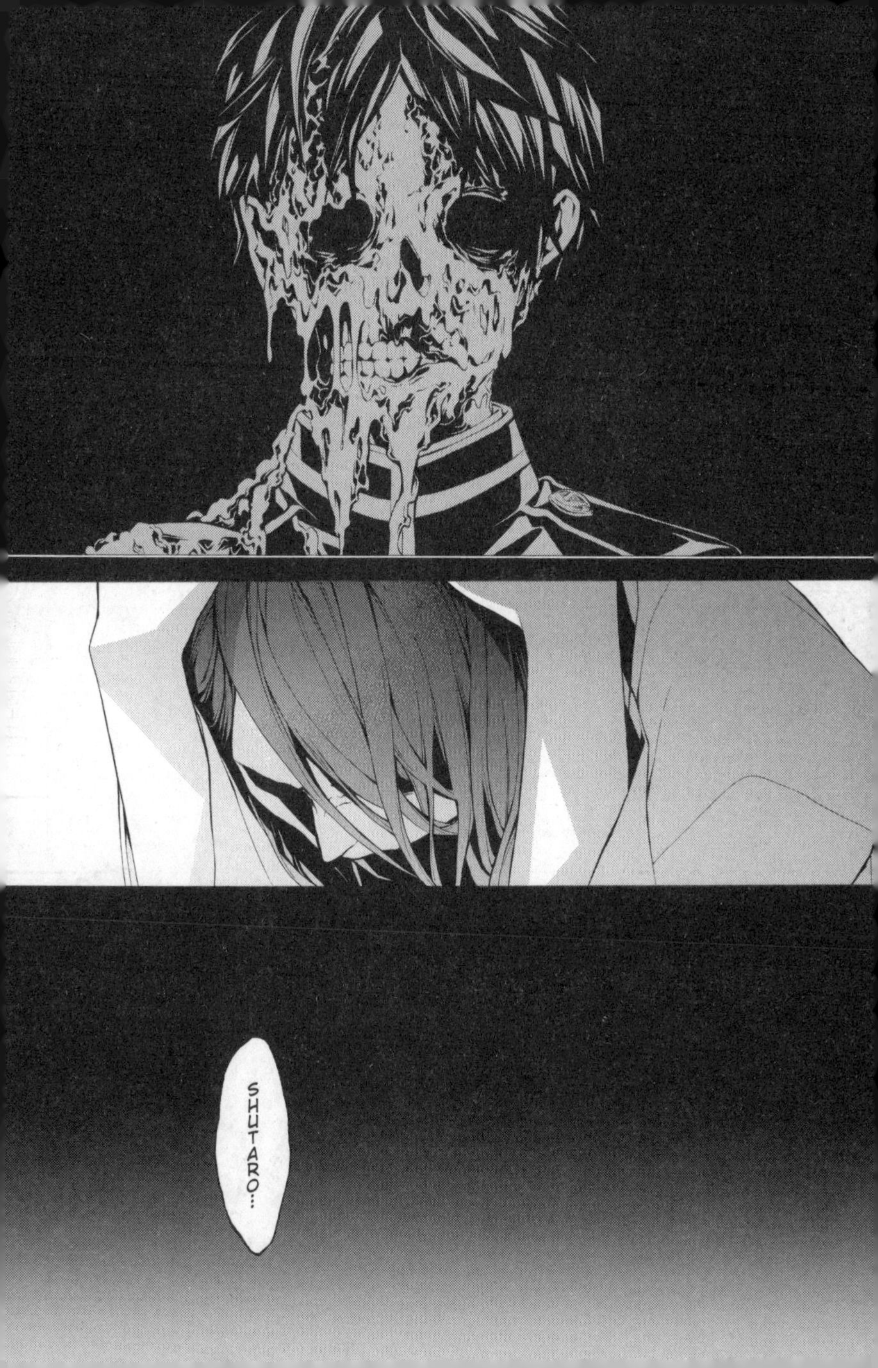
SHUTARO...

Tokyo.
FWIP
Tokyo
Nitto News
The Circus Murders at the Imperial Hotel!!
THE CIRCUS MURDERS, HUH?

THE INCIDENT AT THIS HOTEL IS BEING WRITTEN OFF AS THE WORK OF A SERIAL KILLER, BUT WE KNOW VAMPIRES ARE INVOLVED.
IT SEEMS THAT THE MEMBERS OF CODE ZERO HAVE BEEN RATHER CARELESS.
WELL, NAKAJIMA-KUN?
A MOVIE SHOOT?! I CAN'T BELIEVE THE PUBLIC BOUGHT THAT!
AND NOW WE'RE ON THE HOOK FOR DAMAGES CAUSED BY YOUR UNIT!
THE SUPER SOLDIERS SHOULD BE OUR COUNTRY'S TRUMP CARD AGAINST THE WEST'S GREAT POWERS.
BUT AT THIS RATE, THE NAVY WILL TAKE ALL THE CREDIT WHILE WE, THE ARMY, WILL BE TREATED AS MERE ACCESSORIES. WHAT A DISGRACE!

CARE TO EXPLAIN, NAKAJIMA-KUN?
HOW MANY YEARS HAS IT BEEN SINCE YOU FIRST PROPOSED THE SUPER SOLDIER PROJECT?

CODE ZERO WAS ESTABLISHED TWENTY YEARS AGO.
AND ITS CURRENT STATUS?

SPECIAL UNIT 16 CURRENTLY CONSISTS OF EIGHTY MEMBERS.
FOUR VAMPIRES OVERSEE SPECIAL OPERATIONS.

FOUR ?!
YOU'VE BEEN AT THIS FOR TWENTY YEARS, BUT ONLY HAVE FOUR SUPER SOLDIERS?!

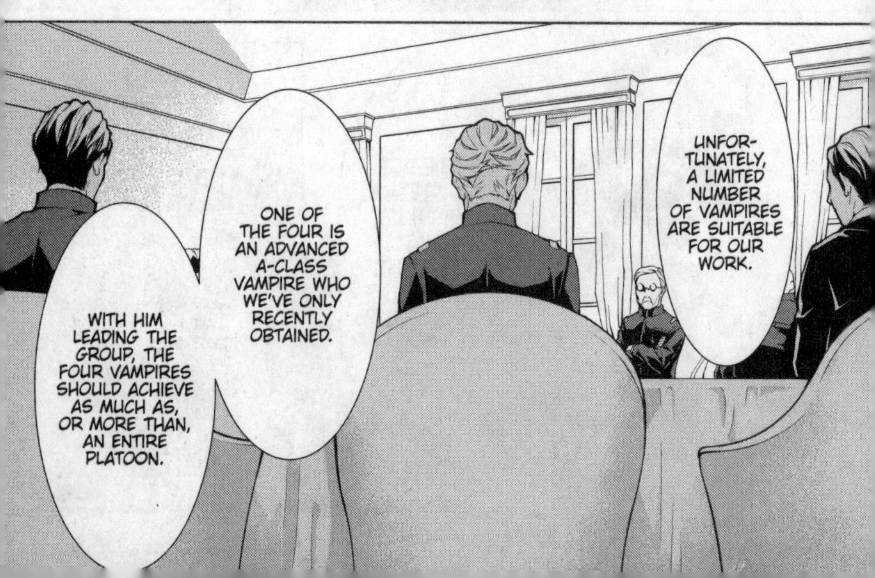
UNFOR-TUNATELY, A LIMITED NUMBER OF VAMPIRES ARE SUITABLE FOR OUR WORK.
ONE OF THE FOUR IS AN ADVANCED A-CLASS VAMPIRE WHO WE'VE ONLY RECENTLY OBTAINED.
WITH HIM LEADING THE GROUP, THE FOUR VAMPIRES SHOULD ACHIEVE AS MUCH AS, OR MORE THAN, AN ENTIRE PLATOON.

AN ARMY IS ALL ABOUT NUMBERS! TREATING THEM LIKE HEROES WILL JUST CAUSE PROBLEMS!
NOW, NOW. LIEUTENANT GENERAL NAKAJIMA IS A WAR HERO HIMSELF, SO IT'S ONLY NATURAL HE'D SEE HIS MEN THAT WAY.
GLANCE
......

THERE'S TALK THAT COUNTRIES THAT LOST THE WAR HAVE REORGANIZED THEIR ARMED FORCES AND SIGNED NEW AGREEMENTS.
I'VE EVEN HEARD THAT SOME ARE DEVELOPING SUBMARINES AS WE SPEAK.

Tokyo
Brawl at the Imperial Hotel
Circus Murders at the Imperial Hotel!?
AND YET, CIVILIANS ARE MAKING A FUSS ABOUT DISARMAMENT!
WE CAN'T AFFORD TO FOCUS ON YOUR SO-CALLED "SUPER-SOLDIERS"!
THE AGE OF STEEL IS UPON US! THAT'S WHAT WE SHOULD BE FOCUSING ON!
WE CAN'T AFFORD TO WASTE MONEY ON FLIGHTS OF FANCY!

GOOD POINT.
PERHAPS IT'S TIME YOU GAVE UP ON YOUR SUPER SOLDIER PROJECT?
WHAT DO YOU SAY, NAKAJIMA-KUN?
THAT WOULD BE A MISTAKE.
I CANNOT ALLOW ALL OUR ACCOMPLISHMENTS TO GO TO WASTE.
WHAT ACCOMPLISHMENTS?!
ALL YOU DO IS MAKE HEADLINES THAT WE HAVE TO CLEAN UP!
VAMPIRES BURN AND DIE WHEN EXPOSED TO SUNLIGHT, CORRECT?
THEY'RE HARMLESS ONCE MORNING COMES!

IT'S FAR MORE PRACTICAL TO FOCUS ON SECURING IRON, INSTEAD OF FUNDING A COVERT UNIT THAT CAN ONLY OPERATE AT NIGHT.
YES, THAT DOES SOUND SMARTER.
HA
HA
HA!
INDEED!

CODE ZERO IS UNDER MORE SCRUTINY THAN EVER.
IT SEEMS SO.
THE PRIME MINISTER WISHES TO CUT THE ARMY'S BUDGET...
WHICH IS MAKING THEM GROW IMPATIENT.
REDUCING ARMAMENTS AND CUTTING TAXES... THE PEOPLE WILL BE THRILLED.
BUT TRUTHFULLY, THE PRIME MINISTER ONLY CARES ABOUT GIVING THE *IMPRESSION* THAT HE LISTENS TO THEM.

YES. EVERYONE SEEMS TO BE TAKING THIS PEACEFUL TAISHŌ ERA FOR GRANTED.
THE WAR HASN'T TRULY ENDED.
EUROPE, AMERICA, AND RUSSIA ARE ALREADY EYEING US AS A THREAT.
THEY'LL ATTACK IF WE SHOW WEAKNESS.
THEY ASKED ME WHAT I THOUGHT ABOUT USING VAMPIRES IN A SPY UNIT.
THAT'S WHAT THEY DO IN ENGLAND, THEY SAID.
HOWEVER, THAT'S POINTLESS.
WHEN I COMPLETE MY SUPER SOLDIER PROJECT, OUR ARMY WILL BE REBORN AND REIGN **SUPREME.**
THOSE WHO HIDE BEHIND DESKS SEE THE BATTLEFIELD MERELY AS A STAGE.
AND SO, INSTEAD OF BULLETS, THEY FEAR VERBAL ASSAULTS FROM THE GENERAL PUBLIC, WHO ARE ACCUSTOMED TO PEACE.
I DON'T THINK I'VE DONE ANYTHING WRONG.
YOU CAN'T SAVE A COUNTRY WITHOUT FIRST SAVING ONE YOUNG PERSON.

YOU SAVED ME DURING THE LAST WAR.
THAT WAS A LONG TIME AGO.
IT MIGHT SEEM LIKE THAT TO YOU, BUT FOR ME IT WAS THE HAPPIEST MOMENT OF MY LIFE.
ON THAT DAY, I WAS LEFT BEHIND IN THE MIDDLE OF ENEMY TERRITORY ON 203 HILL.*
EVERY TIME A BULLET CUT THROUGH THE AIR, A COMRADE WOULD DROP DEAD.
I KNEW I WAS NEXT.
AND AS I WATCHED THE JAPANESE ARMY RETREAT, I REALIZED I'D BEEN ABANDONED.

*A 203-meter high ground in China where the Siege of Port Arthur took place during the Russo-Japanese War.

THAT'S ENOUGH, MAEDA-KUN.
JUST AS I WAS ABOUT TO GIVE UP HOPE, I HEARD YOUR VOICE.
YOU CAME TO MY RESCUE WITH A SINGLE PLATOON.
YOU USED AN ENTIRE UNIT TO SAVE A SINGLE SOLDIER. I BET YOU CAUGHT HELL FOR THAT.
AND AFTER THAT, YOU TOOK ME UNDER YOUR WING.
I'M ETERNALLY GRATEFUL.
I'M ALIVE TODAY THANKS TO YOU.

MAEDA-KUN.
I DON'T WANT THE NEXT GENERATION TO SUFFER BECAUSE OF THE WHIMS OF POLITICIANS.
WE MUST COMPLETE THE SUPER SOLDIER PROJECT ON BEHALF OF OUR COMRADES, WHO HAVE SACRIFICED MUCH TO GET US THIS FAR.
EVEN IF IT MEANS SELLING MY SOUL TO THE DEVIL.
THE NEW RECRUIT, A-CLASS LIEUTENANT KURUSU, HE'S JAPAN'S STRONGEST VAMPIRE.
YOU MUST TRAIN HIM WELL.
I, MAEDA YOSHINOBU, MAY BE UNWORTHY...
BUT I WILL DEVOTE MYSELF TO THE SUPER SOLDIER PROJECT!

ALWAYS SO FORMAL.
I JUST--
Sway
!
IS SOME-THING WRONG?
OH, NO. I JUST FEEL A LITTLE DIZZY.
YOU'RE ABOUT TO GET BUSIER, SO REST WHILE YOU CAN!
Lieutenant General Nakajima!
TAKEUCHI-KUN INVENTED A TANNING MACHINE, DIDN'T HE?
YOU'RE FAR TOO PALE. WHY NOT TRY IT OUT?

YOU MUST BE JOKING.
ON THAT NOTE, PLEASE EXCUSE ME.

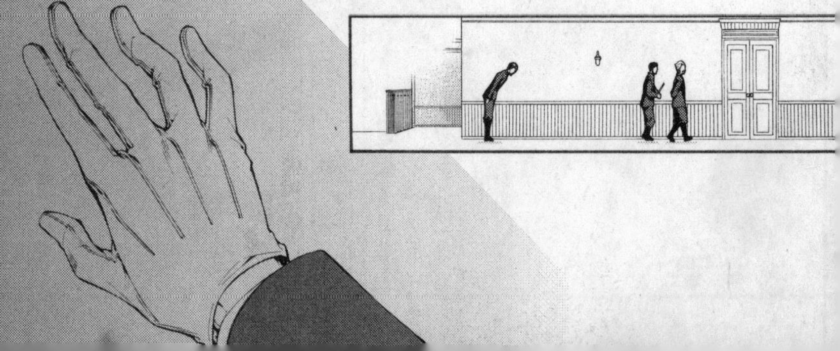

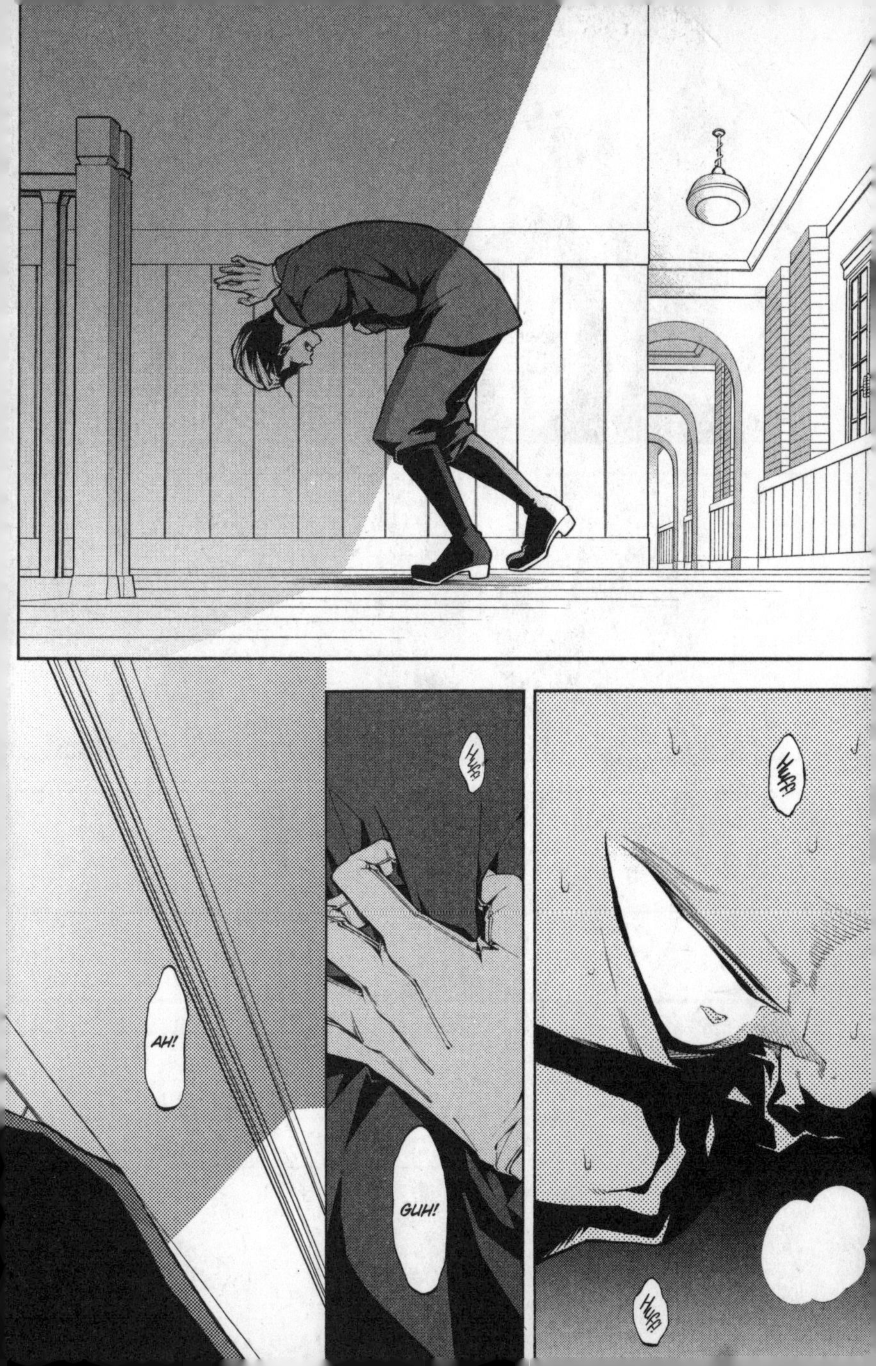

HUFF
HUFF
HUFF
GUH!
AH!

天満屋
Sign: Tenmanya

I SEE. YOU FOUND THE BLOOD MULE, THEN.
HOWEVER, WE HAVE *ABSOLUTELY* NO OTHER LEADS!
WE STILL DON'T KNOW ANYTHING ABOUT YOUR BUSINESS RIVAL.
I'M SORRY WE CAN'T BE OF ANY HELP.
WHAT ABOUT ITS CONTENTS? YOU'VE CHECKED THEM?
WE HAVE. IT CONTAINS THE V-**VIRUS.**
THE VAMPIRE VIRUS IS IN THE BLOOD SERUM?
SHOULD YOU REALLY SAY THAT?!
IT'S FINE. WE HAVE A GIVE-AND-TAKE RELATIONSHIP WITH TENMANYA-SAN.

MORE IMPORTANTLY, SUWA-SAN, YOU JUMPED DOWN FROM A HIGH PLACE AGAIN, DIDN'T YOU?
COLONEL MAEDA WAS MUMBLING, "DOESN'T HE REALIZE WE HAVE TO CLEAN UP HIS MESS IF THERE ARE ANY WITNESSES?"
Tch!
OH, SHUT IT. EVEN IF SOMEONE SAW IT, THEY WOULDN'T *BELIEVE* IT.

TOMIKO.
MINORU.

Sigh...

Siiigh...
WHAT'S WITH HIM?
HE'S BEEN LIKE THAT SINCE WE GOT BACK.

IS TOMIKO-SAN HIS WIFE?
Tomiko...
YES.
BET HE STARTED MISSING HER AFTER HE TALKED TO YOUR CHILDHOOD FRIEND.
SO HE WAS JUST ACTING TOUGH.
IT'S BEST TO LET GO OF ANY ATTACHMENTS TO YOUR PREVIOUS LIVES.
A DEATH NOTICE HAS ALREADY BEEN DELIVERED TO YOUR FAMILIES.

CLATTER
?!
WE'RE PREPARING NEW FAMILY REGISTERS FOR YOU, SO THAT'S THE FIRST STEP.
FROM NOW ON, PLEASE STICK TO THE SHADOWS AND AVOID ANY OLD ACQUAINTANCES.
IT'S OUR LOT AS VAMPIRES.

NGH!

SUWA-SAN, ABOUT WHAT YOU SAID EARLIER ABOUT PEOPLE NOT REALLY SEEING US...
CAN THEY NOT SPOT US EVEN IF WE FLY AROUND IN PLAIN SIGHT?

YEAH, THEY WOULDN'T EVEN SEE YOUR SHADOW.
YAMAGAMI-SAN.
WHY?
LET'S GO SAY OUR GOODBYES.
WHAT?!

PEEK...
NO ONE'S HERE?
WHY THE HELL DO I GOTTA SNEAK AROUND IN MY OWN HOME?
That damn Kurusu!
"WE CAN MOVE AT SPEEDS THAT NORMAL PEOPLE CAN'T PERCEIVE, RIGHT?
"SO, IF WE SUDDENLY APPEAR AND DISAPPEAR, THEY'LL PROBABLY ASSUME THE DEAD HAVE COME TO VISIT THEM IN THEIR DREAMS.

"THIS IS OPERATION: SEE YOU IN YOUR DREAMS!"
SHOULD I REALLY BE HERE?

I'VE LOST A LOT OF WEIGHT.

I GOT TIRED OF EATIN' ALL THOSE BLAND MEALS IN ENGLAND, SO I WAS LOOKIN' FORWARD TO GRABBIN' SOME TEMPURA TOGETHER WHEN I GOT BACK.
NOW I CAN'T EVEN STOMACH THE STUFF.
CREAK

WHO'S THERE?
!

H...
HONEY?
TOMIKO.
SHE LOOKS SHOCKED.
I GUESS ANYONE WOULD BE IN THIS SITUATION.
DID YOU COME TO VISIT ME FROM THE AFTERLIFE?
HUH?!
UH!
YEAH.
SORRY.

YA MIGHT NOT BELIEVE THIS, BUT...
I DIED AN HONORABLE DEATH IN BATTLE. EVEN GOT PROMOTED TWO RANKS!

TOMIKO?

YOU REALLY...
AREN'T WITH US ANYMORE, ARE YOU?

......

I'VE GOT SOMETHIN' I WANNA SHOW YA.
COME HERE.

HUH?
HYUU

I HAVEN'T SEEN THIS VIEW IN AGES.

WHEN THIS PLACE WAS BUILT, ALL THE NEIGHBORS STOPPED BY TO TAKE A LOOK.
THEY ALL WANTED TO SEE OUR NEW WESTERN-STYLE HOUSE.
I BROUGHT IN A CARPENTER FROM ENGLAND AND EVEN HAD THE BRICKS BAKED BY TATSUNO KINGO.*

*Tatsuno Kingo was a famous Japanese architect.

AND YET, WHEN I ACTUALLY WENT TO ENGLAND... MY MIND KEPT WANDERING BACK HERE.
I KEPT THINKING OF THIS HOME WE SHARED.
I CAME UP HERE WITH YA WHEN THEY FIRST FINISHED THE ROOF, DIDN'T I?
YES, YOU DID.
BACK THEN, I WONDERED WHY I FELT SO MUCH HAPPIER WHEN THE HOUSE WAS STILL UNDER CONSTRUCTION.
I...I THINK I ALWAYS WANTED MORE THAN I HAD.
EVEN THOUGH I WAS ALREADY FAIRLY SUCCESSFUL, I NEVER SAW HOW GOOD I HAD IT. I FELT LIKE I NEEDED *MORE*.

I WAS A USELESS HUSBAND AND A FAILURE OF A FATHER.
SO, IF YOU WANT, YOU CAN GET REMARRIED.
I WON'T COMPLAIN IF YOU FIND A NEW MAN.
HONEY...
SELL MY THINGS AND KEEP THE MONEY FOR EMERGENCIES.
YOUR FUTURE IS FAR MORE PRECIOUS THAN ANY MEMORIES OF ME.

I WILL *ALWAYS* BE YOUR TOMIKO.

PLEASE KEEP VISITING ME UNTIL THE DAY I JOIN YOU ON THE OTHER SIDE.

SURE.

I PROMISE.

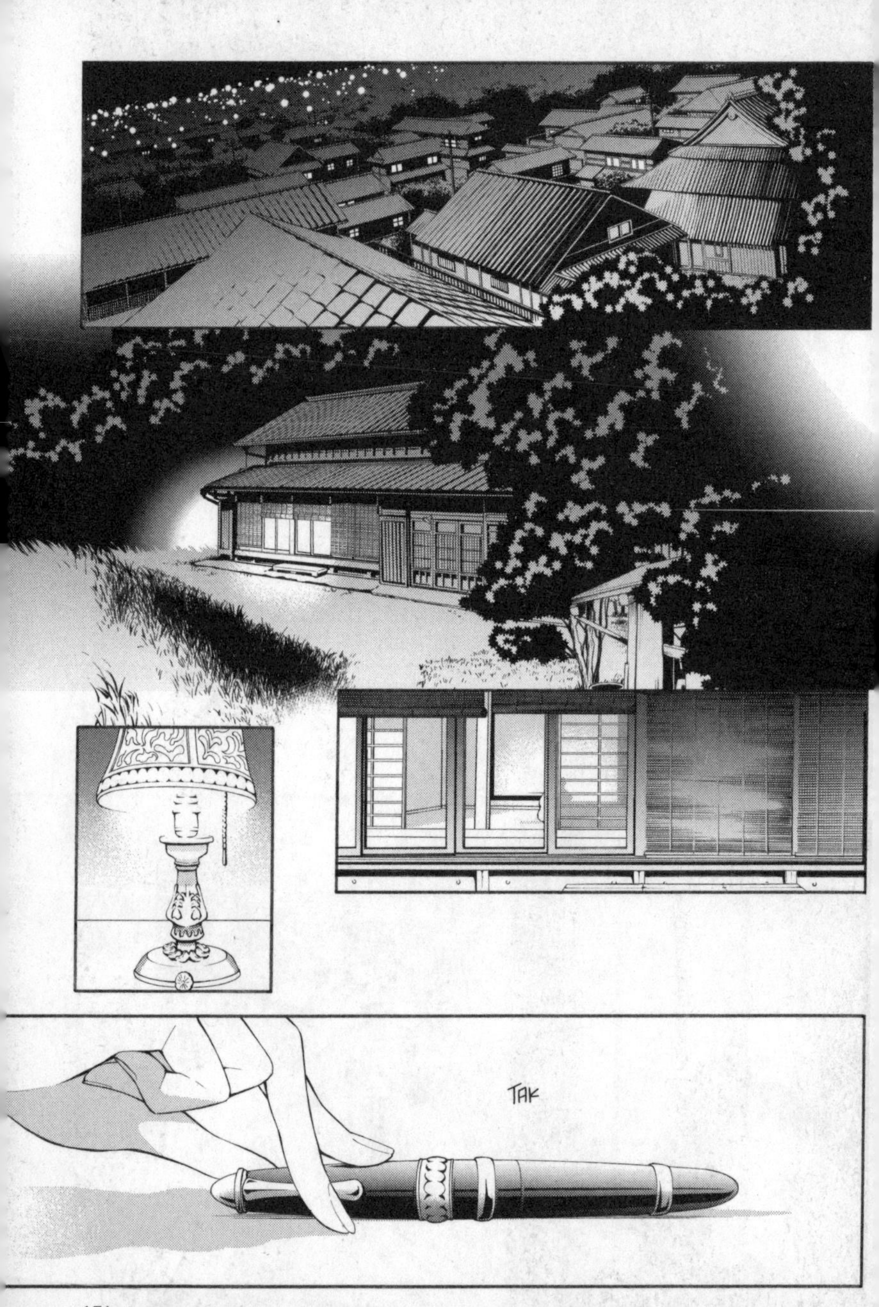
TAK

TAP
TAP
ALL DONE.
THIS STORY'S FOCUSED ON ROMANCE, SO I HOPE THE EDITOR-IN-CHIEF ACCEPTS IT.

Whew

I'VE BEEN PASSING OUT A LOT LATELY. AM I REALLY THAT TIRED?
GUESS I'LL HIT THE HAY EARLY TONIGHT.
CRACK

TAK

FWISH
WILL IT BE BRIGHT AND SUNNY AGAIN TOMOR-ROW?
SHUTARO...

Aoi?
What are you doing?
Looking at the clouds. It's a nice day, isn't it?
Notice of Death
We just got word that Sentaro-niisan died in battle.

He must be in heaven by now.
It's above those clouds, right?
They said it happened three days ago.
What was I doing on that day...? It's the day my brother died, but I can't even remember.
Now you're all alone too, huh, Shutaro?
Sentaro-niisan was your only friend, after all.
My father died, my mother died, my grandpa died.
I'm used to it at this point.
I know I'll never see them again.
It's true.

I'm sure they're--
Still watching over me, even in death?
I'm tired of that cliché.
This isn't a fairy tale. What's he protecting me from, exactly?
What good is it if he's watching me from heaven?!

If there's anything I can do for you...
Just... don't die.
Pretty easy, right?
Okay, I promise.
DIE...
DIE...
AND DIE AGAIN.
Notice of Death
Army: Private First-
Kurusu Shutaro
I WISH WE WERE ALL IMMORTAL.

MMN.
AH?
I FELL ASLEEP?
A BLANKET?

SHU-
TARO
?!
!

SHUTARO?

I'M HERE TO SAY GOOD-BYE.

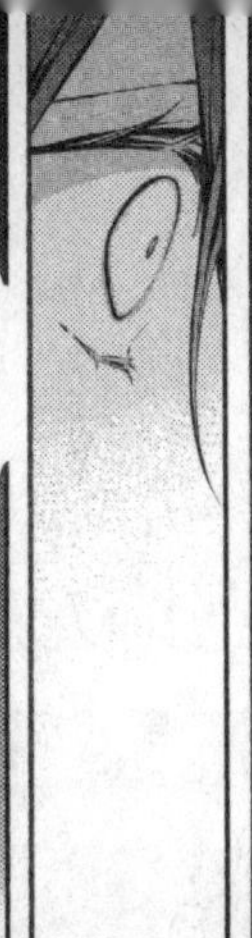
OH.

AND YOU'VE COME TO SEE ME ONE LAST TIME?
ARE YOU AFRAID I'LL FEEL LONELY?

YES.
HM.
CAN'T YOU COME SEE ME FROM TIME TO TIME?

EH?!
WELL... I DOUBT IT...
WHY NOT?

I'VE GOT ORDERS FROM ABOVE, SO...

ORDERS?!
FROM WHO, EXACTLY? BUDDHA?! GOD?!
N-NO! THAT'S NOT WHAT I...! UHHH...

SO YOU'RE A GHOST, HUH? YOU DON'T LOOK VERY SPOOKY TO ME.
WHY DON'T YOU FLOAT? OR RATTLE YOUR CHAINS?
PLEASE TAKE THIS SERIOUSLY.
THERE'S NO WAY I'LL BELIEVE SUCH A RIDICULOUS STORY!!
EVEN IN DEATH, I'LL PROTECT YOU...
DON'T SAY THAT!
HUH?

I ALREADY TOLD YOU, I DON'T NEED ANY MORE DEAD PEOPLE WATCHING OVER ME!!!
I'M SORRY.

TAKE ME WITH YOU!
IF YOU CAN'T DO THAT, THEN KEEP YOUR PROMISE AND STAY HERE WITH ME!
AOI!

HEY, LET GO!

"DON'T DIE"!
THAT'S *ALL* YOU HAD TO DO! WHY CAN'T YOU KEEP SUCH A SIMPLE PROMISE?!

PLEASE... LET ME GO.

....
YOU SMELL LIKE BLOOD.

!
GULP
I HAVE TO GO.
GOOD-BYE.
WAIT!
SLU
MP

I'M SORRY.
BUT EVEN IF I MUST RESORT TO DRINKING HUMAN BLOOD, I WILL PROTECT YOU.

WHAT A NICE DAY.

CAUTION: OVERHEAD

WELCOME BACK.
HOW DID IT GO?
WORSE THAN I EVER IMAGINED.
TOO BAD!
PERSONALLY, I'M JUST GLAD I GOT TO SEE FOR MYSELF...
THAT MY WIFE AND KID ARE DOING ALL RIGHT.
......
WHAT'S WITH THE CREEPY FACE?

HEY, WHERE'S SUWA-SAN?
PROBABLY WATCHING A PLAY.
A PLAY?
YES. HE CLAIMS IT'S ONE OF HIS HOBBIES.

ZWISH
IS MAEDA HERE?!
WHOA!
WELCOME BACK.
HE'S NOT HERE.
WHAT'S WRONG?
DIDN'T YOU GO OFF TO WATCH A PLAY?
YEAH, ROMEO AND JULIET.
ONE OF THE STARS...
WAS A VAMPIRE.

WHAT ?!
WHICH CLASS?
IF MY HUNCH IS CORRECT... HIGHER THAN KURUSU.
I DON'T KNOW WHY, BUT FOR SOME REASON...
AN S-CLASS MONSTER HAS TAKEN UP RESIDENCE IN TOKYO.
MARS RED 1 End

AFTERWORD

Weaklings, thy name is vampire...

I wanted to tell a story of humans who are suddenly thrust into the role of vampires.

Come to think of it, no other monsters have as many weaknesses as vampires. They can't walk in the sun, they can only get nutrients from blood, their sense of smell is too strong, and they sink in water. Plus, the most frightening thing of all is their immortality, which keeps them from spending their lifetime with their loved ones. Even though they've become such monsters, the vampires who still wish to be human are the main characters of this work. Code Zero, which is made up of vampires with abilities that far surpass any ordinary person's, is actually a collection of vamps who wish to remain human.

This is a story that focuses on the physical and mental weaknesses of vampires. However, because they're weak, they desperately try to remain human. So, to me, they aren't monsters, but very relatable people.

This eccentric work, which first premiered as a musical stage reading in 2013 by yours truly, will be adapted into a manga and then animated. I would like to express my sincerest gratitude to Karakara-sensei, who gave flesh and blood to this story, the theater staff, the publishing and anime staff, and most importantly, all the fans who've supported this work. And furthermore, I hope that this story of ephemeral, human-like vampires will bring joy to all who come across it.

Author: Bun-O FUJISAWA

Takeuchi's Secret Tool

Specially prepared blood.

Perfect for when someone can't ingest blood supplements over a prolonged period of time.
Tastes horrible.
If a vampire continuously sucks on one, their characteristic cravings and consequent berserker state can be prevented.

My name is KarakaraKemuri and I drew this manga adaptation of *MARS RED*.

I first got involved with *MARS RED* in 2015 when I helped craft the visual design for th musical stage reading. At that time we talked about adapting it into a manga someday, s I've been looking forward to it ever since. Fujisawa-san's story is extremely interesting and his characters have rich personalities that fit manga well, so I always knew it woul be fun.

However, at the same time, I had some worries.

When I listened to the musical stage reading, I wondered if I could truly express th cast's passionate performance, the music, and the lighting through my art. Fujisawa' musical stage readings are full of energy. I think you'll understand if you're a fan of them

Manga contain flat worlds without any sound or warmth. In that sense, I think they're th most distant thing from musical stage readings, so this might be a medium that fans c musical stage readings don't care for. Some may even have mixed feelings, since th visuals are a different style.

However, I believe they can convey all the same passion. I draw the characters as i they're real. I wonder, "How should I convey this in a manga?", "Is the sound gettin through?", "Does this hit hard enough?", and so on. This work presents many such challenges that I must meet head-on.

I was extremely anxious at first, but the author, Fujisawa-san, was far more lax (in a goo sense), which gave me a lot more breathing room. When I presented my ideas, saying "I want to present it this way in manga form," he'd respond, "That's neat. So, how abou we do it like this here?" He's a very flexible person. It's fun working with him, and I'v really learned a lot.

The original story of *MARS RED* is by Fujisawa-san, and I think the main challenge I've faced while adapting it is how to make the world and characters that hav been lovingly crafted by him interesting in a manga. There are additional parts of thi story that are only available in this version, but all of them are drawn in collaboration wit Fujisawa-san. He also wrote side stories and a background story for Suwa, as well a other short stories to help readers understand the characters better. I'm very grateful.

Of course, we understand that people have been eagerly awaiting this release. W intend to continue to defy everyone's expectations as we continue this story. That way fans both old and new can enjoy it. Please keep reading to find out what happens.

Whether you already know about *MARS RED* or not, you'll find something to like here We'll continue to devote ourselves to making this a great manga.

Also, we appreciate your support for *MARS RED* as it spreads into anime and othe various media!

KarakaraKemuri

MARS RED

Experience all that SEVEN SEAS has to offer!

SEVENSEASENTERTAINMENT.COM

Visit and follow us on Twitter at twitter.com/gomanga/

SEVEN SEAS ENTERTAINMENT PRESENTS

MARS RED

story by **Bun-O FUJISAWA** art by **KarakaraKemuri**

WITHDRAWN

TRANSLATION
Jessica Latherow

ADAPTATION
Maneesh Maganti

LETTERING
Brendon Hull

COVER DESIGN
Hanase Qi

PROOFREADER
Danielle King

COPY EDITOR
Dawn Davis

EDITOR
Shannon Fay

PREPRESS TECHNICIAN
...mussen-Silverstein

PRODUCTION ASSOCIATE
Christa Miesner

PRODUCTION MANAGER
Lissa Pattillo

MANAGING EDITOR
Julie Davis

ASSOCIATE PUBLISHER
Adam Arnold

PUBLISHER
Jason DeAngelis

MARS RED vol. 1
© Bun-O FUJISAWA・SMD／KarakaraKemuri 2020
Originally published in Japan in 2020 by MAG Garden Corporation, TOKYO.
English translation rights arranged through TOHAN CORPORATION, Tokyo.

No portion of this book may be reproduced or transmitted in any form without written permission from the copyright holders. This is a work of fiction. Names, characters, places, and incidents are the products of the author's imagination or are used fictitiously. Any resemblance to actual events, locales, or persons, living or dead, is entirely coincidental. Any information or opinions expressed by the creators of this book belong to those individual creators and do not necessarily reflect the views of Seven Seas Entertainment or its employees.

Seven Seas press and purchase enquiries can be sent to Marketing Manager Lianne Sentar at press@gomanga.com. Information regarding the distribution and purchase of digital editions is available from Digital Manager CK Russell at digital@gomanga.com.

Seven Seas and the Seven Seas logo are trademarks of Seven Seas Entertainment. All rights reserved.

ISBN: 978-1-64827-600-2
Printed in Canada
First Printing: July 2021
10 9 8 7 6 5 4 3 2 1

READING DIRECTIONS

This book reads from ***right to left***, Japanese style. If this is your first time reading manga, you start reading from the top right panel on each page and take it from there. If you get lost, just follow the numbered diagram here. It may seem backwards at first, but you'll get the hang of it! Have fun!!

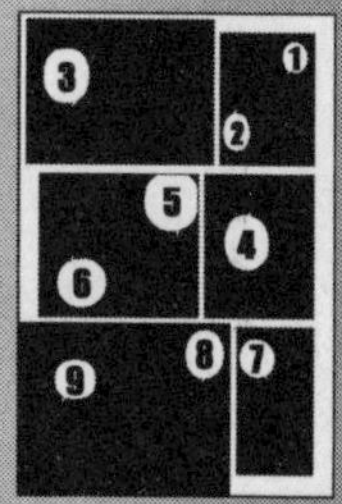

Follow us online: www.SevenSeasEntertainment.com